New Life Clarity Publishing

205 West 300 South, Brigham City, Utah 84302

Newlifeclaritypublishing@gmail.com

NLCP

New Life Clarity Project can send authors to
your live event. For more information or to book an event
contact New Life Clarity Project at newlifeclaritypublishing@gmail.com

Printed in the United States of America

ISBN: 978-0-578-43624-1

MAGICAL CONVERSATIONS

Discover the Magic that Transforms Conflict into Collaboration

By:
Dr Pauline Crawford-Omps

Mission

Harmony between Men and Women to Live, Love and Work Together ...

My mission is to enable men and women to live, love and work in ways that expand their creative output together, especially as changes occur around them and potential conflicts arise. The objective is to convert conflict into collaboration and resolve issues in the boardroom, bedroom, classroom and/or online communication. The intended outcome impacts many aspects of life such as creating deeper friendships, ensuring long term intimate partners, building happier families, developing great team synergy and seeding enthusiastic collaboration in a workplace community that adds a huge return on the bottom line.

If we are to reach these outcomes, we need new rules to replace the old tired arguments that stem from conflict. We need to evolve together, forming agreed principles of trust and respect, women with women, men with women, men with men. With real heartfelt meaning, these principles need to be driven by positive loving values and, more essentially, feed our core belief in human nature to share with kindness and inclusion.

As we all set out to agree on mutual benefits, therein lies the greatest challenge. Are we able to listen without judgment, without anger and without aiming to control others or outcomes? We can only influence others not change them. My passion is for people to share experiences, welcome open-minded conversations, set intentions for magical outcomes, and give permission for all to contribute in a safe welcoming space.

Let's create a mix of love, happiness, consciousness, mindfulness... and playfulness ...and these form our guiding wisdom. In this manner, we can learn to listen, honor and respect each other. When we engage with joy and curiosity, freedom of expression and a wonderment of diverse views, our relationships will grow stronger, deeper, and more sustainable. Wisdom does arrive automatically with age, yet if our lessons of life's ups and downs are learned well, wisdom adds credence to *why we are who we are* as we share in every Magical Conversation.

DEDICATION

To all those who wish to live in love rather than fear. To all who speak their truth yet never seek to damage another's confidence. To a future vision for world harmony and abundance that blesses everyone's life.

PREFACE

This book emerges from my life story. It is a journey of discovery from a mind-logic to a heart-centered existence. Through real-life experiences, I developed values-based principles and endeavored to keep an open mind to everything. I invite you to observe people around you, to engage in conversations that matter to all parties, and to share your experiences in a meaningful way. My lessons learned on the way provide you with substance and practical advice, yet I hope they will make you think and feel differently about your life values and daily communication. I invite you to recall those conversations that have blocked you or caused you upset, anger or distress. Now is the time to release those memories and create a new daily conversation practice that delivers happiness, joy and new discoveries. That's the magic!

Not all conversations will be magical; they may dissolve into arguments, debates, destructive conflicts or even fights. However, with practice, you can create mindful conversation habits by setting your mind to do so and embedding the guidance I share from my own life. This guide is practical and emotional, seeking to set a tone for a conscious and magical future happiness if you so choose. It is less about the words you say and more about the experience you have.

I share my story and experiences and my observations during seven decades of changing times. There are six lessons for you to explore and a story to ponder on for our future collaboration as men and women in a world facing rapid changes. There will be many more lessons I am sure that you will uncover as you journey on in your life. The results will be evident in how you feel as you enter and exit each magical conversation. The goal is for you to get beyond saying, "I'm right, you're wrong" that stops you progressing and take a journey to a positive space and outcome that feeds both your life happiness and your financial wealth.

I wish you well, with loving intentions, please proceed and enjoy the magic!

CONTENTS

Acknowledgments   xiii

1   My Natural Gift to Connect   1

2   21st Century Real-Time Living   9

3   Never Make Assumptions   15

4   Set Well Thought out Loving Intentions   23

5   Know Your Innate Ability to Connect   29

6   Levels of Conversation   45

7   A Formula for Magical Conversations   55

8   Magnetize Your Message and Win Business   75

9   Epilogue: Bears & Birds, Who's in Charge?   85

About the Author   87

ACKNOWLEDGMENTS

My gratitude to all who have inspired me to bring Magical Conversations out of the magician's box at this stage of my life. Special thanks to my daughter, Gemma for officially naming me as one who "creates Magical Conversations" back in 2008, I am honored to do so and am always inspired by her wisdom about people and communication styles. Thank you to my son Ben and my son-in-law Frazer who have both shared valuable insights with me as to how men of their age perceive conversations that matter and why men engage with other men differently to women. Thank you to my two grandchildren, Fin and Georgie, who bring curiosity, many searching questions and a lot of fun to conversations that matter to them. Thank you to my husband Jim for engaging in a special Magical Conversation in 2011 when we met in our first serendipitous meeting in Budapest. His love for me and his belief in my work has brought me to this time and place. I am thankful for all my siblings, parents and my ancestral family, and to my wonderful friends and colleagues, they have all influenced my life's journey of many thousands of conversations. Each one is an intricate part of my story.

Thank you for those in the UK, in Malaysia and now in the US with whom I have had the privilege to connect with, collaborate and work on projects together across a range of businesses and who share my vision for boardroom balance, equality and harmony.

As I have resided, during my travels, on three continents, I have had eye-opening opportunities to observe and communicate with new perspectives from different cultures that are worlds apart. For all these amazing conversational experiences, I am grateful for what I learned first-hand and can now share with you.

1

MY NATURAL GIFT
TO CONNECT

As children, a great deal of what we do naturally sets us up for what we do innately as adults. Those natural creative talents or gifts, born with you, often seem to disappear as you are influenced at school and are guided by well-meaning, or otherwise, parental controls. Valuing your gifts is the key to why you are who you are today. Do you know your natural gifts?

Ever since I was a young girl, my natural gift has been to connect and chat to anyone who would take the time and listen. Another formative aspect that came naturally for me was to be a bit of a tomboy. This made me feel different to many of my girlfriends as we grew into puberty and young adulthood.

During my childhood I didn't really enjoy dressing up as princesses or having tea parties with my friends and their dolls. I much preferred climbing trees, riding my bike, building dens and maybe playing football or cricket with my brothers and their friends. I dreamed of being a sailor on the high seas when other little girls dreamed of being a ballerina. Don't get me wrong… this doesn't mean that I didn't enjoy being a girl; I assure you that as I continued to grow attracted to boys, that attraction was reciprocated. I grow into a love of dressmaking and dancing, family gatherings and parties. The main feature in all my relationships has been and still is connecting people and gaining an easy way of using conversation that helped everyone feel good about being together. I also learned that I did not like conflict and I became good at mediating my way through times when this occurred. I did not always do this well in the beginning as I used an avoidance tactic when I was young. As I grew to know myself however, I learned the magic of an open mind and principles that I will share with you.

I became determined to improve myself every day and had started my self-reflection by the time I was a teenager. This required a great deal of observation, analysis and evaluation. As I traveled this path, I found that my natural gift of connection created attraction and I had friends coming to me, boys and girls, asking me questions about this and that, and wanting my opinion.

Girlfriends wanted my advice on boys, and the boys came always asking for advice on girls. It was as though I could *magically* tell them what they needed. I didn't realize it at the time, but all those elements were gently nudging me to choose the path where my natural gifts were working and my experiences (internal as well as external) eventually led me to be a people developer.

In most ways I consider myself to be an ordinary young woman but one possessing an extraordinary desire to serve people. More specifically, I help others grow their confidence and communication skills. Of greater importance, however, is the nature of my involvement. I work with people to help them determine *why they are who they are*. That may sound convoluted, but it really isn't. In fact, this is my own personal journey down this path... *discovering why I was who I was*... that helped me discover my passion to bring what I learned to everybody wanting to find the answer to all their truly big questions in life that start with... WHY?

It's amazing how much a person can learn through the simple and basic act of observation. It was through observation that I was able to see the variations and individual differences that make each of us unique... that make you, for example, stand out even in a crowd. Why? Because each of us has some very distinct characteristics some of which may even mandate, to a degree, certain feelings into behaviors. The way we express those feelings as we begin to gently, or in some cases perhaps not too gently, add love to the mix will generate key emotions. Let me reiterate, at this point, that I say this based on my first-hand experience.

As a teenage girl I was more than a little awkward, when it came to be understanding my fears, emotions, & feelings core to that of a teenager, issues that were constantly invading my *safe space* during this period in my social development. I didn't understand any more than any other girl or boy my age, and I'm pretty sure this was what compelled to me to develop a look and demeanor that told my peers, "Am I bothered?" Apparently, the message that I inadvertently communicated was, "I know how to cope because I already figured it out." In retrospect, I think this somewhat dismissive and cavalier attitude that I was able convey; initiated by my introduction to new people…who seek greater understanding not just of the world but of themselves.

As time passed, I did what most people my age did… I attended school, traveled around England on family holidays, completed my mandatory education and then went off to university. After graduating university with a dual major in Sociology and Statistics, I found a job at a travel company and set off to see the world, among other things. In the ensuing years I married my university boyfriend, eventually gave birth to a son and then a daughter and became a working parent like my husband at the time.

I am a proud and lively baby boomer and have had many adventures. After I was amicably divorced in my late 40s, I threw myself into my own business which focused on people, work and cultures. My core purpose was, and still is, to encourage men and women to carry a healthy high-performance mindset, be self-motivated to achieve yet connect with each other in a collaborative values-based collective conversation.

I met my second husband, Jim - an American musician and educator - in Budapest over a decade later, in Hungary late 2011 during a conference neither of us wanted to attend. We were then 62 and 67 respectively and had it not been for our love of travel and adventure our meeting would not have happened. I wonder if it hadn't been for our Magical Conversation that he and I had during the breakfast period on the conference second day, we might never have been married within 12 months at a wedding chapel in Las Vegas, Nevada with an Elvis Presley impersonator singing at the ceremony. Since then we continued our travels, circumnavigating the globe in the process. In addition to the countries that each of us has experienced in our lifetime before we met, we lived in Malaysia from 2014 through 2017 then we relocated to the United States, taking up residency in Southern California.

The key lesson I learned from then to now - transitioning from a housewife to an entrepreneur; to an educator to international speaker – is that *people are people* everywhere and many human relationship issues are the same no matter the cultural overlay. My natural gift of *connection* means that I seek to converse so that I can discover more about the other person and build a relationship through that exploration of commonalities and differences. My natural gift is ever present and as I travel to different lands and meet different audiences, the only challenge, across cultures and all diversity, is a person's intention and willingness to grow and engage with me.

I have developed my own self-esteem and confidence over my lifetime, determined to know my value to me and others. My good and bad experiences continue to drive the changes that I have yet to go through and desire to achieve. Core to all my life and shared in my work delivery is **The Value Creation Cycle**. It's a relatively straightforward cycle that influences my whole life. It functions on the premise that only *I* can create *my* value. The *I* - or you might say *'me'* - factor is key, and I teach my clients to be open-minded and take a long...and very objective look in the mirror... literally.

As awareness grows... and it will if you are willing... and you begin to smile and value your physicality, your biology and your cerebral mindset preferences. As you recognize and acknowledge your natural personality, your innate talents will bloom. Only then can you further realize your capacity to add value to relationships and to your life. The 'me' influences the 'you and me' (relationships) and gains momentum for the last part of the cycle, the 'we' impact on their community life. The value cycle creates the understanding that you are responsible for all things in your life. Overtime the magic of life evolves with you in the driver's seat. My number 1 natural gift has given me a skill for life and as my life adventure has evolved, I am now known as *Miss Magical Conversations*!

It is time therefore for you to assess your natural gifts and realize how these are easy to own because they are yours and no one else can take that away or own them. If you embed these into what you do and, trust me, magic will arise. These gifts well used bring you joy and confidence and reminding yourself of the natural gifts you were born with, those things not taught at school, is an essential first step. A simple example is the natural ability to smile. At the age of 17, sitting looking into the mirror, I rated various aspects of my face, eyes and hair. I noted in my diary that as I looked and felt better when I smiled and so I would make that my own gift to my world. Sounds straightforward now, yet it is an element of my presence that is frequently complimented on and adds to the magnetic magic of my presence. It is a gift I have deeply embedded in my persona and is as natural as breathing for me. Everyone can smile, you can too, yet I observe that many do not. They wait for something to smile at!! I even wrote in that diary "I am surprised adults do not always smile and that it was a shame" In my naïve youth I had yet to discover the conflicts ahead that weigh people down and make that smile disappear.

With my clients over the last 3 decades, I have asked them to assess their natural gifts. Through countless seminars and workshops, I find women can be quite dismissive of their natural gifts if they deem them to be less valuable in their workplace experience, such as being a natural cheer leader, a natural inquisitor, a natural word person, a natural organizer or natural caretaker of other's needs.Men on the other hand are often confident of their natural physical gifts e.g. mechanic, artist, footballer etc, yet don't always note the emotional gifts within these such creator, visualizer, dexterous with hands and feet.Natural gifts such being empathetic, being a natural healer, gifted at friendship, known for a kind and generous nature, being an observer and so many more unteachable skills, are untapped talents on any resume or job application. These natural gifts are the most valuable yet often not measured in a materialistic world where you are qualified by your paper credentials. You are not the same as anyone else. Your fingerprint, and you, are unique. Your natural gifts are powerful beyond measure and part of the magic you can bring to your life and especially revealed in your conversations.

Valuing our differences as men and women is another very important factor for conversation ease. The key to getting along better and creating new rules, that are mutually beneficial, is to value the differences that can seem difficult and, if unattended, can dissolve into conflicts and fight. Situations are difficult not people, yet it is easy for you to assume a difficult stance if you don't value differences. I have always been passionate in helping other people connect through communication and conversations that make a change occur. As the change evolves and the collective consciousness of people shifts, I observe the conflict melting and an opening for collaboration. My vision for the future is that men and women natural balance and flow with each other's natural gifts and **create solutions together.** There seems, however, to be many times when men and women just don't see eye to eye, heart to heart, and words and deeds produce confusion and chaos instead of magical outcomes. I use the term *magical* as an energy to allow the *unbelievable to become believable.* Is there a way to make the unreal real and the unknown to be a space to play in?

My intention in sharing my experiences with you to enable you to create Magical Conversations for yourself. Whether you are male or female, of any age, culture, ethnicity or sexual orientation, the choice is that, as a human being, you can find that magnetic magical communication and relate to all as you wish to attract. As you chose to be in control of your conversations (not controlled by or controlling others) you will impact every aspect of your life, your family, community, business and intimate experiences. My intended legacy is to share the wisdom of those who answered the call to become aware and wise, when dealing with the growing demands of the today's world. The territory we all live on is shifting fast and we need to be more aware of the obstacles and blocks where gender mix, the rise of professional career women, the generational merger, the dual income working parents, entrepreneurs and business leaders in contest and cultures clashing can drain our ability to smile. We are surrounded by a social media digital existence that puts everything on show.

My vision is to enable women to listen to the wisdom of men and vice versa in a spirit of mindful loving intention; to allow magic to occur, in the unknown space of all possibilities.

Your natural gifts are born with you, use them to their fullness.

They were given to you and you alone, so you can be successful and happy.

2

21ST CENTURY LIVING

You may scoff at the idea of Magical Conversations...

When you read the news today, it becomes apparent that the general population of the world is still stuck in terms of achieving positive conversations between men and women at the top of the corporate world, the political government arenas and within gender groups, many women's movements, men's groups, entrepreneurial networks, local communities and family enclaves in many parts of our social and domestic world. Men and women alike get stuck into the "I'm right, you're wrong" dialogue and end up either fighting or turning their back on resolutions!

Despite this turmoil I hope you also find a growing groundswell of good stories. Sometimes you must go and search for them, however they are there. Tales of collaboration where men and women creating amazing entrepreneurial and philanthropic ventures work together; of communities recognizing the value of women in the workplace as leaders; of men sharing emotional wisdom and seeking a heart-logic values-based life. Too often these stories are shrouded by nasty stories of male rhetoric and vicious "put-downs" of women, sexual harassment cases and frustrated cries from women concerned about the *bad behaviour* of men, especially prominent celebrity or political figures. It's time to stop this cycle of negativity, this struggle for power, life is a game not a battlefield. It's time to live, not kill ourselves with hate and fear. It's time both men and women distinguish their ripples of magic before we all get sucked into confusion and spin into mayhem and damage beyond human repair.

Is your life engaged in a whirl of chaos and confusion? Or do you sing to the music and dance with life's magic?

You need to step into a new paradigm that says ALL is possible. For example, you can change the conversation and agree criteria that embraces all parties in the boardroom and throughout your working experience. You can orchestrate better conversations at home where tensions in teenage years can get out of control. Stop arguing about "what ifs", e.g. if women were in charge would the economy be better? What is happening to men within this chaos and confusion of the merger of business with emotions? The emotional upheaval in the workplace inevitably seeps into your family, social and intimate conversations. Do you stop to reflect before you speak? What changes does this result in?

I have many clients – male and female – who have doubted their ability to get past a stuck point. One leader, a strong female boss, was troubled by her uncooperative staff and senior leads. Over a period of six months, we resolved the issues by slowly allowing her staff to speak openly within the structure of a Magical Conversation development program. There were component parts to this process. Each person became aware of their natural gifts and combined with their gender dynamics behavior, they came to understand their differences and how to relate to each other. As they shared differences in the context of their roles singularly and together, they found renewed energy and creativity. In a safe circle of sharing, where each was valued rather than critiqued, the whole department became collaborative. *Awareness, acceptance then action* became their mantra and the boss reported that the results in better working together lasted longer than any other development program they had invested in.

That senior team had really believed nothing would change yet it did. In that program, the sessions covered 6 months, embracing 19 very different men and women in an HR department in the UK, typical of many workplace cultures where communication had got stuck. This book is to help you to evolve your own magic, using **'Magical Conversations'** guidelines. Know that you can turn any conflict situation around. You will discover unknown possibilities are available; you will find judgements can be reframed as anger and limited beliefs are shown the door. Your world is changing fast and today is no longer like yesterday. Is it time to change the rules on your negative experiences? Can you use your natural gifts, energize your imagination, seek the unknown and create magic wherever situation you find yourself in? Your only question is "are you willing?"

It is the time to look outside the past restrictions which have created confusion and stopped progress. The WHY seems obvious to me -that living with love-filled values and positive intentions rather than fear- based controls, is the better option. It is the 'how?' that is our challenge. This book is to engage YOU in your personal magic.

Magical Conversations are not soft and fluffy.

They are based on all parties being valued, every parties having an equal right to contribute and everyone understanding and respecting the rules. Ah ha you say 'RULES!' Yes, simple and all-embracing. The rules are simple: No judgments, no anger, no restrictive behaviours, no outrageous or harmful *controlling* behaviours allowed. All parties are to be heard, acknowledgement that not every view is right, and not every view is wrong, but appreciation of everything contributed and all points considered. At the table, no conclusions or decisions are made without consensus or at the very least a degree of observation, patience, perseverance and imagination.

Can you feel the magic? The magic is in the mix of contributors, the choice of topics, plus the agreed positive willingness, energy and commitment to mutually respectful outcomes. In a magical conversation circle everyone wants to be present.

Are people ready to shift their perspectives and be truly inclusive? Many factors come to bear but let me first focus on the gender dynamics to break through misconceptions and inspire a more positive approach. Then magic may occur faster!

For over 30 years I have addressed many lively groups; business men and women, many solo entrepreneurs, many corporate players, many owners of small successful businesses, and my theme is always generally about "living a loving intentional life". My encouragement is that you live a fulfilled life whether male or female, at home or at work. My vision embraces all of you 'taking responsibility and ownership for your lives'.

I am often asked, by female clients, "how can we bring love and energy into their business existence?" as surely the only way to have a healthy lifestyle existence.

By helping you, as a woman, become a magnet and attract wise men to live and work with as business professionals, you serve both yourself and others. I encourage women also to attract wise female support as mothers, sisters, friends, aunties, daughters - and colleagues, as customers and suppliers. The goal is to attract a multi-faceted, emotional, caring, intelligent, highly talented, visionary collaborators for today's future.

Some men may never have been approached with this heart-centered style of living that women desire and can achieve. It's down to you, as a man, to share by your true nature in every communication, while recognizing men and women have core natural differences when it comes to *conversational behaviour*. Today more and more men recognize that the heart is needed to balance the logical mind. This will lead you to more awakened balance. In this state Magical Conversations allow you, as a man, to expand your lives for the better. Having said that, generally men are less likely to have lengthy unconnected conversations. Men tend to get engaged in a topic and lend their views and thoughts focused on that seeking an outcome and a comradery. Women may converse similarly but more often they hold conversations that cover variable topics, personal agendas and go off at tangents, employing emotions more readily than men.

If you take a wise stance on all matters and draw on your natural gifts, you will more easily develop personal wisdom to make you more magnetic and an attractive power source. Your natural gifts, as I have written earlier, are your strength and your power, and are uniquely presented by you to others as you engage in conversation. Your success depends as you *knowing you* as you listen and connect with others. Connection is two way. You may be a male or female from any generation and culture across the world, you may have a strong masculine energy or a softer feminine energy within either gender biology and therefore your core attributes combine to inform the success you have with others. Remember the mantra with my client's story; *awareness, attraction then action*.

Women can embrace men and bring their light to shine, and men can share their wisdom with women to uplift their aspirations, and each can inform, influence and emerge new ways to work together.

My advice to female audiences is to build *collaborative consistency*; play your best authentic card, draw the female baton and hand it on to other women around the world with loving generosity; use your whole brain, left and right; open your mind to changing the limitations, rules and regulations and do not hide as your magic evolves. Let yourself own that special place in the moment and seek to work together with other women to find your voice too. Know that women are not all the same, yet they have the same loving nurturing core whether they become a mother or not, they love to take care of people, spaces and situations.

Women - you have fantastic opportunities now to get involved in business, in politics, in social change and in determining your children's future. Yes, it may be a long road of change, but it's happening as you sleep, eat and go out to work day by day. More and more men and women want a more purposeful world, a world where work and life find a more compatible coalition. Magical Conversations are occurring everywhere.

Men - you have the opportunity now to own your sensitivity and emotional wisdom. I advise men to stay on purpose to be a valued mixture of the masculine and feminine within your manliness. Share your awakened wisdom with other men openly where you acknowledge your sensitivity and creative nature. I am uplifted to meet more and more wise men, of all generations, who think, feel and act in a space of conscious awareness of others in the community around them. Men tell me they want to be heard in a new light, to be honoured for their emotions and allowed to share these without being smothered, to be able to enter the conversation to listen within their own timeframe.

My intention is to set the Magical Conversation ripple circling outwards far and wide and see how far the magic can reach. The lessons that follow are keys to success. They are real life imperatives to not only great relationships and a love-filled life but instrumental in the growth of good business.

Changing Times impact the need for care and attention, so be the change you wish to be. Men and women living loving and working together in harmony.

3

LESSON ONE:
NEVER MAKE ASSUMPTIONS

Right or wrong, they'll always block your flow!

Are your conversations full of magic or do they pour confusion and discomfort into your life? This is a book of common sense and wisdom drawn from my nearly 70 years of communicating. Ever since I could talk, I have been a chatterbox! Reprimanded at school for too much chit-chat and challenged by skilled teachers, family and friends who tell you to listen and learn, I recognize now the true value of a Magical Conversation and the limitations we place on our existence when we speak without setting out to connect.

Without a connection, speaking to someone can be one-way communication. Meaningful conversation is quite different, these turn into magical ones. Whether it's a conversation with a soulmate, a boss, a colleague, a close friend or the checkout attendance at your local supermarket, the conversation experience can be magical and creative or confusing and misleading.

Let's explore what's going on and don't make any assumptions about what will unfold as you read further. It's all about connecting and feeling the connection. When it works, it's magic!!

Have you ever noticed that people who make assumptions and talk loudly on an issue do not generally encourage a flowing conversation in response? They deliver their communication with an affirmative "I'm right... implying "you're wrong".

They don't invite a response yet may demand attention. This is not magic to me. It can turn into confusion, blocks, arguments and, often, a negative experience.

This happened to me one breakfast meeting with a potential contact who I had been watching as a possible resource for my business, a business focused on enhancing people's daily performance through conversation excellence.I had the pleasure of being in his workshop the previous day. His style was what I would call "breakthrough with toughness". I had enjoyed the substance of the program but not his style. I was there as a willing participant and went with the flow but felt he placed me in conflict too readily. As we set at breakfast for the second day's program, he fired questions at me, loaded with assumptions a) that I was there to listen (I did) and b) to 'tell' me how HE was being and how I could work with him.

As the firing paused, and he eyed me fiercely, I set off on a slight tangent to set the scene for possibilities of work. He stopped me quickly with a statement I will never forget "Pauline I don't think YOU realize who I am and how expert I am and... we're not having a conversation, I am talking at you!" I paused for breath, sipped my tea and looked him straight in the eye. I responded: "Your program is excellent (no lie) but whether we work together or not will depend on my client's requirements." I stopped talking, sipped my tea, and said no more. No conversation required and such a good example to me of the different energy force when you're engaged in communication. It's about connecting and feeling the connection, remember? Our relationship was doomed. He stood up, offered a handshake, duly taken, and said "Good we understand each other". I was quite astonished!

I have no idea what he thought we agreed on or understood, I would never work with him. Whether had I been a man, we might have done a deal, I will never know. For me this reminded me of my need for a more inclusive style that I desired for my life and what I did not want. In business terms, this meeting was a failure to connect with no way forward. How often do your one-way dialogue patterns such as this, stop the flow of your business?

Although his assumption and intention may be correctly delivered, (for the speaker) it landed in a straight-line projection on the designated audience and if it doesn't land right, it crashes. The only way to receive an assumption is to agree or disagree, the latter often producing an argument. The former can create a dialogue, which may in turn into a discussion and in the end a lively conversation depending on how you handle the original assumption. If you fight it, then you'll have an argument of debate. If you agree and it's not your view, you will end up controlled. I have long since practiced removing assumptions from my life, however they do creep back when I am not paying attention to the flow I want.

A Magical Conversation is one where the flow is circular, interactive, fluid and no one person controlling the airwaves. When everyone is engaged and contributing freely and without conditions, then creative outcomes emerge naturally. This is a growth potential style for business and for life. A win-win situation.

For every conversation you wish to keep alive, and especially a Magical Conversation, assumptions are a block rather than a good start point. I learned my conversation skills many decades ago, long before there was digital activity adding a certain level of instant gratification and text communication. Now we all used smart phones and social media, conversations are in many formats. What really mattered, in my early years, was uttered in the moment, spoken out loud, and so immediate interpretation available. My best conversations came when there were no assumptions, judgements, anger or external controls. As a little girl who loved to chatter, I gained my natural guidelines early on but often failed to enjoy the experience if my self -confidence was attacked. The perpetrator was often unaware of the attack. If I couldn't contribute useful knowledge, views and ideas (even when I had them) I would stay silent and unheard. I didn't realize, until later in life, how magical I could make my life merely by believing everything is possible, having the confidence to know my wisdom, and valuing a sharing style of talking and listening that became inclusive, compassionate and authentic. Earlier in my life, I wanted Magical Conversations to happen yet didn't dare say what I wanted to say in case of ridicule. At that time, it seemed unbelievable that I would eventually bring my natural chatter to be my future gift to the world. Surely magic tricks are like that? Presenting the unbelievable as believable!

How did this change occur for me to move beyond my lack of confidence? Well it is a life journey we all can take, and whether you are an introvert or extrovert, the first step is willingness to engage in self-discovery and taking the necessary steps to achieve success. Learn as you grow as well as taking in knowledge. Your history is part of who you are now. Value the lessons learned.

For me, born in the age of telephones attached to the wall, letters going via the post and telegrams being the fastest way to send messages, I was privileged to learn conversational skills in a pure and utterly deliciously loving home environment of 'chatter'. In an era where children were told to "be seen and not heard" I was very lucky to grow up in a conversation-rich, happy and loving family. I am born to converse and connect with people, places, design and ideas, use my imagination and grow dreams. I literally have always seen the world as an inter-connected set of elements; me, my physicality, my emotions, my friends, my family, my colleagues, my designs, my ideas, my service nature. I see things in both logical and sequential flows, life to me is a simultaneous *and and* experience of probabilities and possibilities.

Over my lifetime, I have loved connecting the dots. Not surprising to you by now, I was a natural mathematics student, I found happiness in those childhood games where you literally 'joined the dots' 1,2,3,4,5 to a 100 and, as you closed the sequence, the character on the page is revealed. As my maturity evolved, I loved simultaneous equations and started to imagine pictures, designs and scenes without even putting pen to paper, the numbers, dimensions and shapes rose from the page in front of my eyes. I see shapes connected, design in my head, see maps as pictures, lines and spaces aligned and inter-woven into the fabric of every day. These things woke my creativity in dress making from an early age. Constructing clothes was, and still is to me, a jigsaw puzzle coming together. Having the end picture before you start is key. This is how I came to realize what I now share with in this guide to, what I call, the art of Magical Conversations.

As the middle 3rd child of four, I always felt connected in a stream of experiences. I remember so many conversations with my elder brother admiring his handsome lead, my sister forming those close bonds that females create together, laughing and chattering, and childhood games with my younger brother, climbing trees and playing our stories out in the garden tree house in North London.

The most concentrated informative time that I received

'conversational skills' was in my early school learning. This was making connections as I formed friendships in the classroom and playground. I discovered that I had an innate ability to converse and, even though shy, I had an unbounded enthusiasm to be first in attendance every day in my school classroom, so I could meet and greet, listen and connect everyone as required. It was a natural role I placed on myself and it set the intention for my later life when I became a well-known and prolific networker, weaving connections as I created my entrepreneurial career. Now via the internet I can do so even more directly in my global experiences.

At school, I became the source of information, the conduit through which people left messages for others and shared secrets. I became the confidential ear for those stories that needed to share yet I held onto my mission to resist gossiping as is often endemic in girl's schools!

In this time, my early passion to help people help themselves came forth. Being surrounded by a large and happy family, who indulged in many British style tea parties, annual vacations together, and many picnics and fun outings before fast-food joints and smart phones stole our lives, my two brothers and sister and I were encouraged to be familiar with those visitors regularly entering my parent's home. Also taught to be welcoming, we helped in serving others in all festivities, and many times perform a party piece to the assembled audience. As I grew into a gauche teenager, I was always expected to join in, listen and converse with adult aunts, uncles, grandparents, cousins, peers, and a wide range of friends of the family. A rich environment to learn about conversations. As a naïve soon-to-be adult, I listened and learned different styles; some direct, some indirect, some fierce and angry, some soft and gentle. Many assumptions would be aired unchallenged, yet others would provide a lively open-minded discourse on a topic and explore the whys and wherefores of everyone's experiences. The latter were my favorites and informed my mind, my curiosity and my interest to deepen my awareness of those subjects that resonated with me. I was young and naïve yet always keen to learn. I learned early on in life that I did not like assumptions, they always got me into trouble!

When I left home to go to university, I continued to hone my conversational approach. I soon learned that I attracted a wonderful group of friends, pals, mates... boys and girls who were eager to get together and 'chew the fat' as they say in Britain.

My career progressed through the 1970s and 80s through a post university marketing role in a lively young mixed workplace, several years growing my family, two kids and my university boyfriend now husband, moving around the UK, from London to Bristol, to the Cotswold and country life. Here I landed in a small village (population 200) with two young babies, and a whole new existence. I set too to create my conversation network and soon, like my school classroom, I became the central source for connections across two small villages (1000 total population). My role as a connector, communicator and conversationalist was bubbling throughout yet I had not recognized the power of my experience. After moving back closer to London, in the 90s I became an Image Consultant, and Entrepreneur and founded Corporate Heart in 1999. My passion was to educate employers and employees of the nature of healthy high performance and of course Magical Conversations!

As I look back now at my endeavors, the nature of conversation is at the center of building great relationships, teams, and workforces. It is a vital leadership tool as business shifts and emerges into different more communications-based operations. Since 2000, with the rise of our digitally connected world, face-book, Google, social media and global visibility, we converse all the time. Due to generations and cultural diversity, the growth of women into business and entrepreneurial careers, everything has shifted. The *Art of Magical Conversations* is to harness the core of human connection, the words and experiences we share. I fear this has got somewhat lost during our fast-paced profit-oriented world where time is money and conversations may be deemed a waste of action time by some. We don't always respect the time and people we are around. Both home and business can get marginalized into bit-size-texts. Full sentences do not seem to count, and grammar takes a back seat to action while the pleasure syndrome of the 'what's in it for me' is rampant. Have Magical Conversations disappeared because deemed of no value?

In 2008 I was working as a consultant to corporate clients in London and was working across the UK. A self-confessed workaholic, passionate about my work, networking, connecting, conversing, creating attraction, my aim was to encourage my clients to enjoy their natural gifts and perform to their best. My engagement style was friendly, intelligent and full of smiles. I would often become friends with my clients as a natural part of my teaching healthy high- performance techniques. I would often be complimented on my style of engagement. I was happy. I didn't always make the hard sell that others suggested I do. Yet my best contracts came unexpectedly as I conversed with my usual animated enthusiasm. One day my daughter Gemma, said to me after a particularly magical conversation we had had, where whatever I said made good sense and resonated and created an ah-ha moment for her, "Mum, you should call yourself the President of Magical Conversations." the ultimate compliment and I accepted. As I contemplated the title, I decided that 'Ambassador of Magical Conversations' was more apt. I printed a simple business card with that title and forayed out to the London network scene with confidence.

I remember a lovely summer evening, one of those beautiful rare times in London, a barmy sunlight, a rooftop network party. Magical indeed! As I handed out my new card persona, I became absolutely delighted to hear very positive responses. Did the need to enjoy such conversations coming from a desire for the unbelievable to believable? Was life so tedious and regular, or even stressful and draining, that the thought of such conversations an offering that irresistible?

That first time; an all-female audience. So once more I trailed out my title to a networking garden party in Soho, full of seriously suited men and women. As a lawyer client approached, I shared my card, and she expressed her delight as she knew me well. Her lawyer husband approached us and as she turned, and announced me to him, my heart sank. "Surely he will be skeptical about this" I said to myself! In receiving the news that I was The Ambassador of Magical Conversations, he immediately responded affirming that "this is exactly what we need in the law arena". I was bowled over, delighted and excited. What I realized then and since is that people react positively even to the suggestion without knowing what the *magical* part means. They know if their life does not have it; they are sure they need it; they want it and they hope it will be joyful on its outcome. Having gained positive responses from men and women alike, I can assure you even the mere the idea of Magical Conversations intrigues and delights people from all walks of life.

The time has come for me to act on my discovery and over the last decade I have run workshops, seminars, and programs on Magical Conversations. I now have a decade of experiences, workshops and magical conversation circles to share with you. I bring you not just the *Art of Magical Conversations* but the principles, values and mechanics to ensure it works for you every day.

Make no assumptions, tell no lies, in the moment always be alive to the unknown, the impossible and the magical, to make possible all that you wish for.

4

LESSON TWO: SET WELL-THOUGHT-OUT LOVING INTENTIONS

Do you want a conversation of love or fear?

If you focus on the two core emotions in all conversations, you will notice LOVE (positive) and FEAR (negative) rule your thoughts, words and deeds. Your core quest in starting, joining or ending a conversation is the intention you bring and to what goal or objective you have for both the conversation content and flow and the relationships that occur through your actions. In reviewing your conversations, what emotions do you face more often; LOVE or FEAR?

Interestingly; both LOVE and FEAR produce results and will influence decisions. FEAR, however, damages the user/abuser as well as the abused, but the abused user will, in most instances, be the more adversely affected. More than that, a destructive conversation is not magical and can be renamed as an argument or fight. What is the most likely outcome for you if you allow *loving* to dissolve to merely *liking*? It may be OK for a while however it may decline to *disliking*, falling into *loathing* and moving towards *hating*. That conversation journey takes you to a fearful place.

The power of choice is within you whenever YOU choose love or fear as your guide. The ensuing emotions compelled by LOVE are positive because they come from being in a loving intention state with another human being. These emotions include joy, passion, compassion, respect, trust, empathy, and authenticity… you can continue to add any positive adjectives you identify with. These augment the possibility of a mindful, conscious, loving, living and meaningful conversations that attract magical results. In short, your enhancement is the art of keeping loving intentions alive in you and your conversations, aligned with your values shared with others.

You are "in charge" of your state of mind, body, heart and soul and the choices you make every time you enter a conversation with the intention for magical outcomes. In my experience, understanding life runs on these two emotions love or fear, and all emotions derive from these. Your choice is the key to your happiness and, ultimately, success in most things you want to achieve.

Magical Conversations are underpinned with loving intentions even when focused on serious matters. You can only grow within the core of your being when you are in a balanced, harmonious, mindful, and loving state. Surely, you want to have loving, Magical Conversations, don't you? All else originates from this core to dissolve and freeze fear out of your life. Is this possible? In my experience and in considered opinion the answer is **YES!**

Conversations happen all the time, some are mean, deliberately caustic, angry, and even vicious and deliver chaos and confusion – others are joyful, funny, loving, embracing, creative and achieve magical outcomes. They range from street smart, common sense to high-brow intellectual reasoned and innovative – yet all with the intention to connect and contribute value. The content of a Magical Conversation is the richness of life and delivers results for everyone that are abundant and flexible. Everyone wins in their heart even when taking away different outcomes.

You need to start with valuing where your conversation starts -i.e. with you. Who are you in every conversation? "Before I get to know you, I must know me". This is not an ego pursuit but a self-discovery and knowledge of "who I am" in any conversation.

You didn't arrive in this world with any words. Babies learn to talk over the first two years, some early some late, yet all the time they hear words and are involved in a non-verbal conversation with their parents and family. Especially their mom. Instructions are heard and indeed understood in the first months. As a baby you learned how to elicit responses by crying, laughing, holding on, feeling the touch of another human being. You receive and understand dialogue long before you say your first words. Your value creation starts right at birth (and in the 9months in the womb) in your journey as a human being.

BEING "ME" is your start-button for value creation. This is the "I am..." factor. Set the intentions to get to understand yourself, truly and honestly...and that's not always easy, it means taking ownership of your natural loving value, your physicality, your emotional gifts and your conversation nature. You are the magnet for attracting Magical Conversations to you.

Maybe, like me, you spent much of your early life lacking the courage to own your conversation as a naïve teenager. Distinguish what you perceive and know yourself to be. You may have listened too often to advice from parents, family, friends and colleagues who see you through their eyes, not yours. Your early experience is key to your awareness and ultimate acceptance of your natural conversation style.

Although I always loved to connect and chat with school friends, if I felt awkward and clumsy, made a mistake, or got reprimanded at school, I instinctively believed it was because I was not very clever, hence my self-esteem and confidence suffered and so did my conversation flow. In analyzing my situation as I grew into early adulthood, and in working to overcome my limiting beliefs, I began to realize that being honest with others...and particularly with myself, about what I did not recognize was as powerful a confidence-builder skill as any learned qualification. Instead of carelessly opening my mouth to talk, I started to listen and learn more about how to interact in ways that engaged and flowed. I became the magnet!

Conversation is a journey and as you travel on the road ahead, it will unfold before you with YOU as driver and passenger. As you grow in confidence, never stop listening but do know the "I am..." without ego. It is important you understand that, with a good start, the journey should begin to flow towards recognizing and naturally inviting other people to engage in 'your' mutual conversation. The conversation now 'ours' must embrace all involved or else it's a monologue. It's not about the words as much as it is about the feeling, the experience and the flow of relating. This increases your magnetism.

You might be asking yourself why you need to relate to another person as you build a conversation. It's more than communication, it is about making a connection. Like electricity, you must place the plug into the socket to find a live connectivity. *Relating to others* is a natural input and output of making that connection into a truly magical conversation. It is a great way to develop a lasting relationship. Who do you want to build a relationship with? How do you go about initiating a new relationship? Where would you begin? When will you be able to tell that your conversation is moving into building a relationship? Are you ready to risk your heart by building a relationship? So many questions... so much unknown at this point. The only person you can truly know is YOU and this is a life journey. More on *how to do that* as we progress on our journey.

KNOWING "YOU" – once I know ME (the "I am...") then you need to get to know YOU i.e. the other person/people and build the *connection* mindset for a Magical Conversation. Remember keeping a loving intention in your heart is the easiest way to understand the other person you are talking with.

Seek to understand and value every person you wish to know well and aim to learn new things about them in a loving manner. It is important in your efforts to understand other people that you set your loving intention before they even appear. The "I am..." magnet you are creating by being truly aware of yourself is stronger as you open your heart-center rather than head-logic. Your thoughts matter before any word or deed is shared, however your heart is where your feelings ripple from. How YOU value who you are in conversation starts at home, with your family and close circle of friends. The nature of your conversation value to others is vital if you are to add value back to yourself. This is **The Value Creation Cycle**: 'I–you–we' created with the intention to flow towards the full *together* 'we' conversation and from there into shared outcomes that can build deep and lasting relationships.

SHARING "WE" is where the full magical conversation flows into the 'we' outcomes. Take time to sense your joy in the fullness of Magical Conversations in the collective, in the group and even larger audiences. Sounds simple doesn't it. But I sense you might be saying to yourself, "My experience is different. I set expectations and they fall short of reality once

I get to be acquainted with someone."

The key is to know yourself, unbiased and unfettered (difficult yes?) and set INTENTIONS based on loving thoughts, feelings, words and deeds (do you practice this daily?) and to REFRAIN from setting tough expectations. Try this, please, and see for yourself.

Set INTENTIONS come from your heart, your desires and your imagination. This is what I call being heart-centered human.

EXPECTATIONS come from your head, not your heart, and often affected by external forces, i.e. what others tell you.

In my own personal journey, **_The Value Creation Cycle_** has guided me always to take responsibility for circumstances positive or negative. It is based on an ancient Buddhist principle that I discovered when reading Tsunesaburo Makiguchi's book "Education for Creative Living" His educational experience in Japan over a century ago, showed that young children blossomed more readily and were more creative when they valued their own natural gifts and brought those to play in the way they built value for others and so grew value for the communities. Often your natural gifts are downplayed when you enter the classroom and traditional teaching methods replace your value with a curriculum.

This value cycle philosophy has been a major element in my life success and has enabled me to attract great relationships that are alive, sacred, loving and loyal to this day. This is part of every client session and program that I have delivered over 30 years.

As I applied this in my life, I decided to take responsibility for my thoughts, feelings and deeds every day, dealing with positive and negative conditions with loving intentions - so that I am the master of my own destiny. Everything started to transform as I held this cycle in my mind's eye and in my heart and acted on it. It is my mantra for everyday living.

Three steps...

1. BEING **"ME"** Get to know yourself in every aspect of mind, body, heart and soul, know the "I am..." that you are born to be.

2. KNOWING "YOU" Grow your awareness of others and know why you attract Magical Conversations with another person or group.

3. SHARING "WE" Bond together as you form relationships beyond the boundaries, collaborate, communicate, create our world.

Value the I am within you, be at peace with others, welcome them with joy, know their true value looks you in the eye.

5

LESSON THREE: KNOW YOUR INNATE ABILITY TO CONNECT

Connection levels vary with your Relational Quotient and 4Rs

Your words are important however your tone and delivery, body language and commitment to be present in every moment are vital as breathing is to life itself.

Know thyself is key; the "I am…" starts the "You are…" leads to the "We are…" Knowing others and understanding differences are the richness of relationships and setting the collective intention is vital for an outcome valued by all.

You may be a one-to-one person, more introvert personality, or a one-to-many stage presence, more extravert persona. You may be a mixture of both depending on the situation. Always tune in rather than tune out.

Are you an introvert and avoid conversations? Or an outrageous extravert and over play your role?

How do you relate to you? How do you relate to others?

How do you react to people, places and possibilities?

How do you take risks to step outside your comfort zone and risk possible ridicule?

What overall responsibility do you take for your impact on others in conversations?

Let's develop your RELATIONAL QUOTIENT with 4Rs

RELATE-Ability: *Knowing the value of* WHY you are WHO you are

How do you RELATE to YOU?

What is your current self-assessment with regards to the positive intentions to honor yourself as the man or woman you are?

Are you a tough, strong, aggressive, football-watching, macho man, or a gentle sensitive man, are you bold or shy? Are you the outspoken, ballsy woman, or the quieter gentle protective woman? There are many variations of *gender dynamics* types, however our quest right now is to observe how YOU relate to you and others on an everyday basis.

Are you the type that loves conversations but doesn't listen? Or the one who always listens and then regrets they didn't say anything! Are you someone more focused on *telling* or *asking*? Are you naturally *judgmental* or more of a *perceiver*? Are you a *detail focused* individual or a *big picture-don't-mind-the-details* person? Many will have experienced filling out profiles that outline your personality and temperament. Type and temperament are extremely important ways to recognize differences and the start point to learn about YOU. In addition, if you take a long honest review of your natural gifts, look in the mirror quite literally, take a stock of your feelings, accept compliments when they arrive, and know that you are unique - *and so is everyone else.*

In all cases, your ability to speak, your willingness to engage and your sensitivity to others are primary attributes for creating Magical Conversations. Relax, don't push, allow the pull to your magnet in a positive loving manner.

I accepted that I was a chatterbox tom-boy when I was young and loved talking. As a maturing woman, I knew I was growing into a natural masculine-minded female. Logical and practical in my head, and preferring often to stay there, I was and still am a bold business woman who is always confident, especially in work mode, and, at times, perhaps a little intimidating!

I learned not to be afraid of what I didn't know and how to admit it if the conversation was making me feel overwhelmed. Now I'm alright with all my characteristics because they are mine. I can ask when I don't comprehend something. I temper my natural style with my intention to have Magical Conversations that flow. I learn new things every time I have a conversation. My journey has been to engage with my heart-center while honoring my masculine mind logic.

Today I am stepping up on stage to inspire the world harmony as **#MissMagicalConversations.** I am so much more aware of the factors that everyone can now employ to ensure these are daily occurrences. My experience is here now to help you. If your days are fraught with draining debates, contests on your integrity, reduction of positive affirmations and you are excluded from lively conversations, then start now to relate first to your own style and then learn ways to change your conversation habits.

Start with you:

- Be more aware of your own uniqueness and other people's differences. I balance my conversation strategy instinctively to engage with others as I get to know them. I always retain my authenticity but allow for their style to shine too.

- Know that everyone has a blend of the strong and the soft, the straight talking and the soft more abstract approach. Seek to use the words *tell* and *ask* appropriately especially when different gender dynamics are at play. Men and women are different and we each respond to words and personalities in an emotional way, positive or negative. Owning your emotional response is key to Magical Conversations.

- Develop connections at different levels, practice conversations in small ways before you get tangled in larger conversations that may trap you. Chat with the assistant in a shop, build a mini conversation, see if you can make them feel important to you and find a simple connection. Be genuine.

- Maintained a high degree of self-confidence. I was known as one of the best connectors in business and with family and friends yet in some new situations I would buckle to fear and shut down.

Pamper your confidence daily with affirmations, gratitude and compliments.

I unlearned and unpacked why and who I was during my life many times. Many years after my divorce, I remember reaching a state where I was no longer afraid to be on my own without a significant other. I wrote in my journals, consistently and intentionally to keep my confidence blossoming. You need to love yourself, in a selfless and not selfish manner, to fully embrace the magic you can attract in conversations and therefore relationships.

At my 60th birthday party in May 2009, I was blessed by the attendance of my grown-up daughter and son, Gemma and Ben, my one-year-old grandson Finlay, my son-in-law, Frazer, and my 91 years mother, Muriel. In addition, I greeted a room full of amazing friends. I was single, divorced and very happy in my own skin. I looked young for my age, I smiled that day with genuine love and affection for all those who were a part of my world and I liked *me for me* and for all that I was blessed with. My mother gave a short speech and said I was a "women of substance" and was enormously proud of me. I was fulfilled on so many levels that day.

Over the years I have systematically peeled back the layers to love my tom-boy nature and live my truth as a mother, as an entrepreneur and a world adventurer. I am caring and giving while still being true to my strong, logical business persona. I leverage my natural personal and professional work focused on the science of Gender Dynamics and my own techniques for helping men and women communicate together. I love to work with real-life situations, adjusting concepts appropriately to everyday situational changes. I never stray from my passion, purpose and vision to spread Magical Conversations wide and far.

Here's my strategy for relating to BEING "ME"

Awareness Is the First Step

Your approach to RELATE-Ability is the start-up fuel for your journey to become more aware of your conversational role in life.BEING "ME" is best when consistent in all your relationships and your conversations. My guiding mantras for "I am... ME":

- **Me**– love and honor yourself, know your passion and purpose and use this to attract others

- **Me and you**– love and respect partner love and honor friendships

- **Me and my family**- love and nurture love for parents and siblings

- **Me and my community**- love your friends and socialise with love

- **Me and my world**– love and empathise with a mindful love for the communities around you and the world…

Three **RELATE-Ability** Practices:

1. An Attitude of Gratitude Diary

Get yourself a lovely notebook and a decent pen that you keep precious. Every day, every evening, hand write your gratitude. I am thankful for everything both big and little. Dr John Demartini was the first stage presenter I heard talk about this in the 1990s. He has written his gratitude every day since a young man and built his success on that activity. The power of handwriting your gratitude, the commitment to making a contract with yourself is key. It can be that, on a low day, you merely state a gratitude for being alive.

2. A Book of Intentions

Another notebook, this time for your intentions. You can combine the two… no hard and fast rules… yet it's powerful to have a separate book, as this is for stretching your imagination and your desires for life such as dreams, for far-away places, wealth, wisdom, or good health … and of course for your loving intention to have Magical Conversations every day!

Write down your dreams and ideal goals for your life. Weave a magical tapestry of what you see, hear, feel, sense and desire in your conversational future. You can continue this practice always and encourage others to do so and share ideas and dreams.

Nothing happens by accident although you may need a lot of practice to get to know yourselves and remember you always have free will. Set intentions and watch life reveal naturally!

A Healthy Mirror Image

Take a good review of your current image:

- Get a scrap book, or maybe a coloured envelope file, and pull out cuttings from magazines to collate, select colors and images that appeal and inspire.

- Collect clippings and notes about your life style choices, colors and shapes you like, the places and pictures you'd like to own (or perhaps already own), the dwellings and settings where you want to connect with other people and Magical Conversations to grow.

- Take a good look in your own mirror, take ownership of your body shape, your age, your health, your weight, your fitness level, your style. Get to like your natural birth right.

- Change what you want to change (not with plastic surgery though), get the advice of a sensitive image consultant and/or life coach.

- Make some colourful changes to your attitudes and your wardrobe adding zest to your personal style. Your accessories may be the best starting point.

- Loose or gain a few pounds to find your optimum happy-with-myself weight.

- Remind yourself that in loving me (in other words... learning to love yourself) you are not looking to become egotistical, but humbly honest and truly grateful. True, loving, self-confidence is genuine, authentic and just the way you are, and becomes easy to share sensitively in your Magical Conversations.

- You need to look in that mirror and be perfectly OKAY with who you are. and why you are that way.

- Write down a long list of selfless "I am...." Statements about you and your natural gifts.

My advice is to be completely honest and realistic and give yourself permission to laugh and cry whenever you wish. I have done this so many times in my life. My mantra is "If something feels wrong, it probably is." I can take ownership and make choices. Feeling good about WHY you who you are is essential in your journey to Magical Conversations.

RELATE-ability goes hand in hand with REACT-ability… the next element in our quest to know yourself

REACT-Ability: Your Reactive Communication Preferences

How you react to others is a critical factor when you meet people and enter conversations. Many highly emotive conscious and unconscious elements occur when you meet others and as you get to know others and share from your heart.

Be honest and look at how you react naturally, it is born with you and an important guide to why some relationships are easier than others. You have learned many reactive modes through your early nurturing years from 0-7 beginning at home with family, parents and friends, then at school with teachers and peers. Your communication style will be a combination of what you're born with and what nurturing has taught you to use. As an adult, you can become pro-active and use a conscious thinking and speaking manner. "Think before speaking" is a phrase my father taught me as a child.

Do you tend to react with your left brain (more facts and form) or your right brain (more feelings and future focused)? Have a ponder on what your first reactions are to these statements, I was privileged to work with Dr Asma Abdullah in Kuala Lumpur. She shared her extensive researched techniques with me on communication styles. Here I share a few simple top-level ideas drawn from her work to help you. As you read below, you are probably drawn to one. You may be two or more - or a balance of all four of these.

What is your primary preference when facing any situation or conversation, are you:

- **Facts focused** … you always start with facts and tend to focus on information transacted rather than feelings

- **Figures and Form focused** … you need a process or a formula for every process and enjoy things being orderly and in the right place

- **Feelings focused** ... you enjoy using emotion-filled responses and heart-tugging words, and sense emotional states in others

- **Future focused** ... you look to future possibilities, have dreams and desires, use your imagination and sometimes seem ungrounded

Reflect on how you react right now to all the people in your life. Notice how others who are different to you are communicating. Observe your own style and how others have different styles to you as you mix and match styles together.

A few clues to follow:

- In a conversation, your REACT-Ability may be a clue to un-resolved differences that could undermine your conversation. Understand and review your own reactive communication patterns especially under stress or tension. This time spent in observation will be key to your success.

- Don't make assumptions about others REACT-Ability style until you have an open conversation about their preferred ways of reacting. Do share your own preference with others through sharing experiences and how you approached each. If you are a Facts person talking to a Feelings person, you may not get buy in if you stick to the facts only. Use feelings words to attract and connect.

- Don't place unspoken expectations on another person before you know them or even when you do! Unmet expectations are often the core issue for many conversation breakdowns.

- Ask yourself: Do you truly think you can change someone else? You cannot. Are you entering conversations with expectations set in stone?Please do not, you will fail. Bring ideas, intentions and an open mindset.

- My suggestion (and practice) is to refrain from making any assumptions, judgements or expectations.

- SET INTENTIONS ONLY and share these with others right from the first meeting. "My intention is to get to know you.

INTENTIONS are never wrong (unless the intention is to attempt to change others and that is indeed an expectation!). If you are doing this right, you will find your choices, words and deeds come from your heart. What does your heart desire? What do you value? What will your shared passions be inside the conversation?

It is often expectations that others have of you that harms you during your lifetime. Most of us have had these experiences, whether at school, at a university, in your first job, or from family and friends, when others say; "Do this!" "Don't do that!" These are the result of another's perspective of you ... not necessarily yours.

When you are ready, the conversation will always have the potential to be magical from the outset.

The connective tissue between you and others exists. Your success will be the degree to which you are willing to meet others in the mix.

The personal keys to stepping into Magical Conversations in the best way are:

- Authenticity and genuine inclusion in conversations. Don't wear a mask.

- Alignment of words and deeds. Believe in sharing to learn and evolve.

- Transparency and confidence in self disclosure. Feel safe sharing your experiences and exploring new ways.

MY PERSONAL MAGICAL CONVERSATION OF LOVE

When I met my husband, Jim, in 2011, there was an instinctive attraction for me with him, a relate-ability factor when I met him. We had a magical conversation that sealed our destiny. At that first meeting, because I knew myself well, I was happy not to be swept off my feet romantically. As a practical woman, with a soft heart, and confident persona, I wanted to attract someone who valued me for my intelligence as well as my looks and personality. He valued me, and I valued him, two different personalities around the table of love. He is more feelings first, form second, I am more feelings first and facts second and we both have some future thinking for good measure!

Use Your Words and Actions in Alignment with Your Style

If you present yourself authentically and genuinely, with words and actions that are aligned, you will easily open the door to Magical Conversations.

If you have worked on your own defined **RELATE-Ability** and **REACT-Ability** and are sure about YOU, all else will follow.

RISK-Ability: Your Leverage with Magical Conversations

RISK-ability is an important factor to expand your magical conversation style to engage people especially if as well as being a magnet to attract others, you're genuinely seeking to monetize your conversation's results.

Be the one who sets the different tone, creates the irresistible space that others are attracted to and embrace fully the loving relationships you gather. This will start to magnetize your message (you) and lead you to successful monetizing a win in a business conversation or set the scene for a deal to be made and sealed.

Successful business is always built on good relationships and connecting on a personal level. You might have a fabulous and meaningful product or service to sell of course, but your big successes will be drawn from clients that see your magical ability to make them feel magical too.

RISK is always a factor in relationships, yet once you experience the look, feel, sound, and behavior present in a truly magical conversation, you will not want to lose this state. Don't push, allow the pull – the magnet – to work for you.

Remember, the following can either undermine or enhance your journey as you navigate your way through conversations and the ensuing relationships you build:

- **Change** – is inevitable and *healthy* if you see it that way,

- **Uncertainty** – is the root of opportunity because everything is up for grabs,

- **Victimization** – is a learning moment if you turn YOU around and stay positive,

- **Adventure** – is the spice of life ... both scary and thrilling at the same time, and

- **The Unknown** – invites the essence of discovery, without fear, if you focused on loving intentions and positive outcomes!

RESPONSIBILITY: *Your Capstone to Owning your Success with* Magical Conversations

RESPONSIBILITY is the most important underpinning factor especially when you are setting out to expand your Magical Conversations to embrace a relationship, community or business opportunity.

Everyday chaos and confusion turn up, choices need to be made. Is it easy to give up the magic or will you stay on course when something knocks you down?

How do you deal with the changes in your life to date? Life pressures have changed enormously, for men and women now facing work and home life emotional stresses combined.

Personally, my experience is that many men dislike emotional change, more than most women do but don't talk about it. For both genders, the necessities of life and work - raising families, diverse conditions and multi-cultural influences on all relationships - have both advanced and drained our potential to maintain a firm grasp on daily Magical Conversations. For men, engaging with emotional ease is a sometimes a strange territory. As a woman, more drawn to overt emotional outlets, females can support men on their emotional challenge by sharing in Magical Conversations on the same 'together' agenda. Women can acknowledge men's need for solutions as the conversation progresses. Men can allow for fluid flows and often non-sequential lines of thought from women!

Taking RESPONSIBILITY, in this context, is not restricted to its commonly understood definition i.e. the state or fact of being accountable. In this book, I invite you to be responsible for your personality and the natural assets you were born with. This will help you share more into those Magical Conversations as you lead from your heart-center not always your head-logic:

- Know what you excel at, and what you enjoy doing, what makes you smile, and what are you naturally passionate about doing. And then… as the world-famous Nike ad says so eloquently… JUST DO IT!

- List those things you do naturally and with ease. Do you write, sing, dance, cook, draw, listen, talk, persuade, design, operate, make, mend, connect, question and research? Are you action oriented, quiet, loud, detailed, big picture focused? I am not referring necessarily to learned skills but more about those things you do naturally as men and women …and own it. Do what you love, it will ignite passion and help you find purpose and so be clearer about your vision for life and be able to share these in magical ways. These are your natural gifts – you were born with these not taught them, remember?

- Don't try changing others to adopt your talents and natural skills. Do, however, inquire as to theirs. Love them for their natural talents because, therein lies their treasure trove. Make it your goal to find the common ground that you share and the different talents you can add to your conversation, so it flows wider and deeper.

Taking RESPONSIBILITY is not always a comfortable task when emotions are getting tense or relationships are breaking down. You can use a magical conversation approach as a wise invitation to others to release their resistance or fear. Your responsibility is always to seek inclusion, create and maintain connections without controlling, undermining or suffocating others.

This is the capstone of your Relational Quotient– to take RESPONSIBILITY and use your sensitivity and knowledge with loving intentions to connect at a heart level.

Keep these 5 value statements alive by taking RESPONSIBILITY for the …

1. **Open mind set**– I always respond positively to situations as they arise

2. **Choice**– I choose my intentions daily and write/verbalise them everyday

3. **Ownership**– I know who I am and open to sharing and aligning values

4. **Respect**– I am kind and genuine with all people even those who behave badly

5. **Empathy**– I listen to understand other people and embrace their views

Your Relational Quotient is a combination of all 4Rs – RELATE-ability, REACT-ability, RISK-ability and RESPONSIBILITY

Try this exercise -

Take a piece of paper, and on a scale of 1 thru 10, where **_1 = NEVER and 10 = ALWAYS,_** rate yourself on each of the 4Rs. You might even want to ask your closest friends to score you as well:

RELATE-Ability
I don't RELATE easily to others… I RELATE easily to others

REACT-Ability
I don't REACT well to everyone… I REACT with sensitivity and sensibly to another's style

RISK-Ability
I won't RISK being open and honest… I will always RISK being authentic and honest in conversation

RESPONSIBILITY
I don't take RESPONSIBILITY as it is too challenging… I take RESPONSIBILITY for all my words and actions

Total your score to find your **_Relational Quotient._** If your score is less than 25 points, I invite you to both **_say and do_** the following:

1. "I _will_ improve upon my low scores." List what you are going to do to make this happen.

2. "I am willing to let go of negative feelings and biases." Identify what you will do to reduce and eliminate these.

3. "I am willing to practice the creation of positive thoughts and actions." List ways in which you will achieve this goal.

By the simple act of writing them down, one is far more likely to follow through regarding making the desired changes in behavior.Make your commitments in this way. Please take this little exercise seriously. I will also ask that you be as specific as you can be. If you do, you will be amazed at the result.

My many hundreds of clients who have taken this 4Rs test and found themselves with an under 3 have been amazed at how a simple test broken down into these components can shift them back onto the path of positive thinking. One client claiming a score of 40 was surprised when I said then grow higher scores! The limits we place on ourselves are far greater than external controls. Take time out now to reflect on what you can do next to increase your scores.

I recently received an email from one of coaching clients from 4 years ago saying she has found my 4Rs the most pivotal exercise along with *The Value Creation Cycle* philosophy and yet being in a difficult time in her life, had not acted on the actions and had only now gained a sense of what to do. She said it had changed her life then even though waiting so long for the light to shine. When the time is right, you will know what to do.

React well-informed
about who you are,
take a risk, and know
responsibility lies within
your grasp. Go with the
flow. Don't debate, relate.

6

LESSON FOUR: LEVELS OF CONVERSATION

Principles to prepare for Magical Conversations

From transactional to transformational, from functional, mechanical and operational through to emotional, intuitive, artistic, and visionary, conversations vary. Recognize the innate factors that influence each person's unique style and the conversational gambits that evoke mindful, joyful expression of good feelings and pleasure through to the ignition of imagination and mutual excitement.

You learned about your Relational Quotient. Be okay with yourself. Know WHY you are who you are. More than that, be honest with your emotions and appreciate the perceptions and perspectives of others. Ask those who know you well to share their perception of you. This is a powerful exercise and one not to taken lightly. Ask for three descriptive words about your style of communication and conversation and generally about your natural style. Do not ask people who obviously dislike you. Take the positive words and write them randomly on a piece of paper and see where similar words connect. Allow yourself to see the patterns emerging. Offer to do the same in a group situation, it is a powerful sharing and promotes good feelings. Let people discuss other's perceptions of you too. The more you add positive descriptors, the more you will live into these perceptions. Place your won too about yourself, allow others to compliment you and receive these graciously. My team clients love this process as giving positive feedback to others is often a lot easier then to yourself. It swiftly builds good collaboration and of course Magical Conversations, all of which will add to business performance and results. A win-win for all concerned.

Seek Magical Conversation rather than *mere* communication.

- Recognize when to control and perhaps adjust your words, deeds and realities to the extent that others will be able to see that you are working to understand them. Willingness, practice and ultimately wisdom, will emerge as you build a loving intention into your words.

- Practice your 4Rs and continuously work to keep your Relational Quotient at its highest level.

- Knowing **WHY you are who you are** and **how you are PERCEIVED by others** are the **two** important keys to sharing with others.

- Ask others, especially those who love you, how they perceive you, invite them to give you three descriptors, thank them without question and note the responses.

- Enter your Magical Conversations with intent to connect and build meaningful relationships, whether for business or social life, family harmony or intimate love

- *NOTE: Self Love is not in an egotistical pursuit but is developed in a Value Creation manner where you effectively own your positive loving nature. Your success is not about how others say you should be, it's about WHY you are who you are*

9 Value Principles to guide you

In my journey I have invited many individuals, groups and classes to share their most meaningful relationship Value Principles that underscore the natural creation of Magical Conversations. Let me share these collected pearls of wisdom with you. You should know that I have factored these words of wisdom into my daily practices to enhance my own value creation cycle. These key on the behaviors that I know can own and use to empower individuals, male and female alike, wanting to build meaningful relationships.

I invite you to add your own, of course. I have found these principles work for me, but feel free to alter or edit them to fit your unique persona or - as I just said - you can compose your own. Conversation is part of your life and each one of us has a unique perspective that contributes to the journey we're on and to those we meet along the way. It starts with YOU! Remember that if you remember nothing else.

These principles are an integral part of my intention to lead a loving intentional life regardless of the nature (positive or negative) of those I touch along the way. Whatever you do, make your intentions positive, honest, and believable, making certain that they align with your values... those that **you** live by. These emphasize the characteristics and behaviors recognized largely as an unteachable life attributes... ways of being, own them, live them... so that they resonate with you. They have a direct impact on your becoming and being a loving person, true to yourself and consistent in your world view of love. Through understanding, adopting and applying these principles, men and women will be better able to come together to share Magical Conversations.

- **Authenticity** – Always be honest with yourself. Once you have mastered that, it is of equal importance to **be yourself** always.

- **Empathy** – This aptitude calls for the highest level of emotional intelligence you possess. You are asked to be able to share someone else's feelings or experiences by imagining how it would feel if YOU were in that person's situation.

- **Trust & Respect** – Without respect, trust will not come easily if at all. Your goal is to be trusted first and respected because of earning that trust.

- **Perception** – This is a belief or opinion - perhaps even shared by several people - that is based on how things seem to be. It is not necessarily factual.

- **Perspective** – Everybody has a particular way of looking at or considering something and everybody has that right.

- **Balance** – Achieving a state where all aspects of your life have equal weight and force. When the scale is tilted, something needs to be adjusted.

- **Transparency** – The quality of doing things in a vulnerable way without secrets. Always be lovingly honest and open rather than guarded and mysterious.

- **Clarity** – The quality of being clear and easy to understand. Be sure to understand both what is said and - of equal importance – to that which may be communicated in non-verbal ways.

- **Compatibility** – The art of being able to exist, live together, or work successfully with someone else. Using loving intentions as the embodiment of this seemingly lost art… will create lasting relationships where none existed before.

The Art of Magical Conversations

With these 9 Value Principles in mind, let's explore how we might build a natural connective dialogue resource, holding our beliefs as roots for positive foundations not dividers on our journey of sharing. *The Art of Magical Conversations* aims to maximize your probability of success and the goal is to flourish and thrive (not just survive) through your communicating via a deeper understanding of you and others. There are four further aspects to consider.

Passion, Communication Choices, Assets, and Vulnerabilities

It's time for you to communicate and radiate your passion, communicate with impact, assess your assets and be aware of your vulnerabilities.

Your key to success is to keep learning about your style of thinking, feeling, behaving, sensing, acting and reacting as you meet, relate to maintain and nurture your relationships.

Take Stock of Your Current Situation

PASSION

- What makes you buzz with excitement?

- What are you doing or thinking of when your smiling and happy?

- Are you indoors, outdoors, in nature, in the city, by the sea, with people, one-on-one, surrounded by people, places and possibilities that make you feel good?

- What drives your purpose and vision?

Don't present a story-book version of yourself and do not try to be someone else. Be honest, be authentic and be natural. Share your passion, your motivations and your purpose with those you are interested in.

CAUTION: offer such information in bite-size portions to avoid the proverbial information-dump. Express yourself with sincerity... from your heart center and intuitive guide. Smile, laugh, enjoy and be at ease with who you are, keeping in mind how the other's passion and happiness occurs.

COMMUNICATION CHOICES

- Are you introverted or extroverted?

- Do you converse easily, or are you shy? Are you able to be open and honest?

- How do you communicate instinctively?
  In addition to what you say, are you aware that you communicate non-verbally too?

Develop the channels and environments that best suit your style; the spoken or written word, music, flowers, outings, quiet environments or noisy venues. Pick your favorites and share with your guests. Learn when to stop and listen, and when you listen, invest your full attention. Be authentic, be kind, loving, observing boundaries, especially in the early days of a conversation. Work on developing a no-boundaries, unconditional conversation style by opening yourself up so that you implicitly and explicitly invite others to let go of their boundaries too. No boundaries, by default, implies no judgements, no assumptions, and no resistance opens the possibilities ahead, whether business or personal, be authentic.

Practice being relaxed in your own skin, take a class that helps you tune into your body, such as Yoga, Zumba, Thai Chi, Qigong, Pilates. Feel comfortable with your arms and legs, sitting or standing, be welcoming with your body language.

With my clients in workshop mode, everyone practices and explores these activities together - from formal handshakes to table top meetings, standing on stage or chatting over a coffee, be focused on an open body language, good eye contact and using your hands to support your message (not waving controls) as you host with your own personalized Magical Conversations style.

ASSETS

- What do you do best?

- What are your natural talents? *"I don't have any,"* is NOT *an acceptable answer, we spoke of natural gifts at the start.*

- What have you enjoyed doing? What are some of your achievements?

- What are your values? How do these influence you as you journey ahead?

Don't be shy. Be proud of your accomplishments and list them out… and I'm not talking about your bank balance! Don't brag about wealth even when making a deal. YOU are your greatest asset. The personal you. Be honest with your personal balance sheet. Be interesting as well as interested in others natural assets. Please, this is not an ego trip, you're not guilty for being talented. Assess your natural attributes. Do you draw, sing, dance, cook, garden, write, compose, etc.?

VULNERABILITIES

- What happens to you under stress?

- How do you cope with rejection?

- What blind-spots are you aware of?

- Who do you turn to for support?

Don't hide away. Give yourself permission to be vulnerable, but please do not be a victim. Learn from your potential dark-side and look for the light. Failure can be a powerful learning tool in business, in life and in loving relationships. Through rejection or a personal disaster such as departure, illness or death, our positive practices, knowing and articulating your value principles and understanding who you are as a man or woman, can help you overcome anything. Your own death is the only final exit from the self-discovery journey. Match your actions with your intentions as you choose to overcome vulnerabilities. Hold on to an abundance mindset. There are always more choices for staying positive even through negative situations.

Your **RELATE-ability** is maximized when you are in alignment and fully aware of your PASSION… that which set off your value creation cycle adding fuel to your PURPOSE and VISION.

Your **REACT-ability** is the energy that harnesses your maximum communication impact. Remember, your goal is to develop conversations not just dialogue. Conversation only works when it is a two-way, three-way or more-way!!! You are then truly engaged with each other and your wider community.

Your **RESPONSIBILITY** is to acknowledge yourself by becoming a practiced, principle-led person. Actively work to put the principles into daily practice with the goal of transforming them into daily habits. Your Value Principles will support your progression and enable you to connect, flourish and thrive as a loving person.

It is imperative that, even as you recognize and honor these elements as a daily practice of loving intentions for yourself and others. There is always a potential **RISK-ability** aspect regarding engaging with others. Why? Because you will always have to face the uncertainties created by their VULNERABILITES too. You have the inherent power to cope with change, facing a wide range of obstacles and challenges from ill-health, financial issues, family tensions, divided loyalties, rejections, accidents, up to and including the death of a loved one. It is not unusual for such events to occur, and there is no doubt that they can be difficult to conquer.

Be prepared to meet difficulties head-on for your own sake. Value your **passion**, understand your best **communication skills**, value your natural and embedded **assets**, and bless your **vulnerabilities** as lessons to learn from as you journey onward.

I led a Magical Conversation Circle in 2010 with 12 highly accomplished senior corporate players, six males and six females, plus a facilitator to support the flow, a sensitive intuitive male. The evening was hosted in the boardroom at my top client in central London at the time. The topic on the table was "How does gender balance work in business today". I had carefully invited a range of males and females to share on this. One of the females, a major PLC bank C-suite executive, was going through a personal crisis at the time with her own board and, unknown to me at the time of the invitation, was feeling marginalized herself because of her gender. Her vulnerability showed up at one point as the conversation flowed onto the imbalance for women in senior roles charged with old-fashioned controls.

The safe space of the conversation circle enabled her to express her emotional concerns and feel good about the vulnerable situation she found herself in. Her gratitude to the circle was spoken and applauded by all. A great lesson was learned about being able to be honest with emotions in a business context. If her board had used the same process, they would not have lost a talented senior player. She soon left the post and was head hunted into an even more prestigious board in an international company, one of the most famous in the world, Virgin.

Be passionate, choose well, make wise choices favor positive results, and value the principles that open the gateway to your magic.

7

LESSON 5:
A FORMULA FOR
MAGICAL CONVERSATIONS

The rules of the game

Having worked with many groups and individuals, be assured of one major fact, you cannot force anyone to create or be a good contributor to Magical Conversations if they do not want to. Willingness to be present, without ego is key. Now, you may be thinking, surely everyone has an ego especially in today's cut and thrust material world? It all depends whether it is a healthy self-confident loving ego. I have written earlier of the necessity to know, honor and love yourself unselfishly. This state is key for the following magic to occur. Having a strong dislike of conflict, I had over my life had to deal with such and developed my rules through good times and not so good times.

The rules I have discovered in my own life, that bring about the inclusive style I desired, contain no judgement, no anger, and no-one forcing controls on actions. These became my rules. I have mentioned these earlier in this book however let us get certain of these and the context in which they are embedded. I call them *rules* because these are not up for discussion. Once anger hits the table, then the conversation changes. One may feel angry/strongly opinionated about a topic and there are many in the world to be angry about. Poverty, natural disaster, wars, killings, marginalization of women, male suicides, the list is long. The Magical Conversation disappears *as if by magic* when anger is expressed against another in the circle of safe contribution. This destroys the possibilities ahead. It can be a temporary anger and managed by the circle. To become a Magical Conversation Certified Host, a deeper level of facilitation is taught for serious topic conversations and aligned with a range of *difficult conversation* techniques. The goal is to focus on creative outcomes and mutual benefits where the circle bonds and finds deep trust.

The facilitation of non-conflict resolution methods can be employed and the absorption and melting of anger or any other negative emotion can be managed. The use of Magical Conversations is primarily to invite people to a safe, creative space and to share contributions and allow the unknown and innovative to flow. If anger rises, the conversation might continue as a fight, argument, a discourse, a lecture... whatever it is, it is not a Magical Conversation and so loses the positive benefits.

To ensure that the magic continues, the rules are observed, shared, honored and adhered to. The proactive nature of Magical Conversations means the host or initiator (you) gives encouragement to all participating to develop values of mutuality and interdependence. Your priority is to listen, and give permission to others to speak, second is to tune into the environment, the situational issues, and group personalities. Remember there are no difficult people, there are difficult situations of differences misunderstood, and opinions at odds.

If you practice in small ways, meeting people during your day with this intention to listen and share and connect, Magical Conversations will pop up everywhere in your day. As you meet and chatter, remember you are all partners in the success of the conversation. Check out your *conversational space* you find yourself occupying i.e. could be *in the boardroom, the bedroom, the kitchen or the coffee shop, online or face-to-face.*

The goal, therefore, of these rules is for Magical Conversations to be open minded, joyful, and flowing fully – the experience of the heart not the mind. Make them part of your life, as I have, and welcome the benefits daily. You will attract amazing friends, clients and communities. I am blessed to have done so especially over the last decade of practicing every day the principles and ideas I share here.

This is about real life, real world issues, your life, your conversations, your desires and your dreams. It's not a conversation style learned in a classroom or in an academic text book. The unteachable skills are evolved by your commitment to the life you want not what someone else demands.

Your Pot of Gold at the end of the Rainbow

You walk into a room, your eyes meet, you connect, you click! There is a spark of *inner* recognition and connection with love, with friendship, even with colleagues and clients. There might be 100 people in the room, there might be 10, but the number is irrelevant. It is the fact that there are men and women around or near you. Some will glide past you without notice and without acknowledging you. Others may nod or greet you briefly out of little more than politeness. Still others may stop and chat or engage in a lengthier conversation. As you walk down a street or enter a building or board an elevator, you are able (if you choose) to connect with people. It is the experience and the feeling first that matters more than the content.

An anonymous quote says, "There are no such things as strangers, only friends you haven't met yet." The point is, you are virtually surrounded by hundreds or thousands of people, especially if you work in a city, run your own businesses and even live quietly in suburban neighborhood. Whether on social media or face-to-face, use the same guidelines shared here. You are acquainted with many, several on a first name basis, and a number more intimately as friends and family. There is no shortage of people in your world… people that, should you choose to, you can get to know better. Why is it you will connect with some and not with others? Is it magic?

Believe in love and magnetize your message using your heart center, not your head logic.

For me, those are magic words. It is your heart not head that will take you to the final stages of success regarding Magical Conversations and you will become a magnet for your own success. How you make the magic mix work for you and the other people is 5% luck, and 95% the magic you create. So, you see, Magical Conversations are up to you.

This is what I consider the core i.e. using love and heart centered words and actions, sharing with loving intention in all your conversations to be authentically connected and in tune with others. A successful relationship is always possible if you know why you are who you are, and that the magic, and it is a real, exists in love not fear. My core wisdom is that love strengthens all that is good in my world. Simple? Common sense? Yes, as far as I'm concerned. You need to decide, having read this far, why you choose love over fear, why you trust in *you*, and whether you believe that holding loving intentions for many people in today's world is possible for you in business as well as in life.

The path of loving intentions is not always a smooth one... not always strewn with rose petals there in the land milk and honey. The loving intentions I hold dear and have experienced in my own life to overcome fear, sadness and conflict, were revealed through facing the unknown, experiencing the flow, and at least taking a swing at the curve balls thrown at me. Knowing that I start my value with 'me' and not in a selfish fashion, the "I am...."in a truly selfless manner. Being 'me', knowing 'you', sharing 'us'. Remember the value creation flow; I YOU WE...

And while learning from those elements, I was still responsible for knowingly, appropriately and completely nourishing the companionship, care, trust and magic that only comes when you commit yourself to trust in the universal magic of love and practicing the principles I shared earlier.

A Magical Conversation Partnership

I'd like to share my personal role models for all I am and achieve today. I am truly blessed.

My parents lived a long, love filled life that included a marriage of 62+ years, from 1939 until my father passed at age 91 in 2001. My mother's only love since age 21, she lived another 8 years after he passed away. Although always missing him, she loved her life. She loved life and her life defined love and friendship. She never stopped loving him and feeling his essence around her. At 93 she realized it was time to go to him. They both defined, for me, the magnificence and exquisite nature of loving each other unconditionally. It wasn't always perfect harmony I am sure, still their love for each other and their lives each day, was unquestioned and an example to all who knew and loved them in return.

Their Relational Quotient was high and not only did their love ripple life around them, it was consistent and built on a well-practiced set of values-based principles, behaviors, words, thoughts, beliefs and deeds. Over their lifetime - post 1910s - they had experienced a world war, industrial revolution, social change and the start of the digital revolution, all while bearing and caring for 4 children, in a home large enough for an extended family. They always lived with eyes wide open, a compassionate heart, strong family values and a joy for service to their friends and local community. They always noticed the rainbow.

One Saturday morning recently, I awoke with their memory and a picture in my mind.

My soulmate Jim and I had had one of those days prior where an obstacle had raised its head and we had fallen out badly. A sign that loving intentions are present in your conversations is when such an occurrence comes without you losing site of the rainbow. That was my waking thought. Instead of going to the trash can and throwing your life away, take heed that these moments are precious gifts. I started to draw. I drew a colored rainbow and some grey clouds.

As I imagined the Magical Conversations I desired to resolve our issues that Saturday, I recognized that it takes sunshine and rain to create the magical colors; the whole spectrum from red to orange, yellow, green, blue, indigo and violet. Interestingly, Jim, who is a musician, recalled a song recorded by the Oak Ridge Boys titled "It Takes A Little Rain." The lyrics of the chorus were: "It takes a little rain, to make love grow… it's a heartache and the pain… that makes a real heart show… if the sun always shines… there's a desert below… it takes a little rain… to make love grow."

In the rain clouds you see the dark issues gathering strength. The wind huffs and puffs and blows hot and cold (depending on which climate you're in) and then you get stuck in the *stuff of life*. As I expressed this to Jim that morning, in my drawing, we realized that when we got stuck in stuff, we were arguing in the dark clouds and rain and the despair we might be struck became irrelevant when we stood together and felt the rainbow's energy surround and lift us. Set intentions to recognize when stuff got in the way did not mean that he and I could not tackle issues, but it gave us a space to speak our truth and not be offended; to listen with an embracing heart even with tough topics!

The clouds can contain issues, major or minor. Those listed on my drawing were commonplace topics such as money, trust, friends, family, relationships, inter-dependence, and intimacy in love, differences and perspectives on business and life.

Yours may be personal to your intimate life situation, but the process is the same in business boardrooms as well as round the family dinner table. Recognize when it's merely a cloud and do not destroy your rainbow. We found our pot of gold that morning and ever since when challenges arise.

These can be challenges in work conversations as there are in everyday home life, as today with men and women and technology changing the nature of working, we find life and business merged today. You may well get caught in the stuff of business; the deal, the money, the operations, the control, the pressure to win. The business becomes fragile when stuff takes precedence over people and feelings. Even when the business is seemingly robust, bad relationships and dysfunctional conversations can make or break a deal or undermine large operations. When you build Magical Conversations into the fabric of your business, you and those around you will bring forth the best results.

I was coaching a senior male client in British Telecoms, in the UK, who had presentation nerves. A shy man and 6 foot 4 inches tall, he would present as a willow tree, bending to the wind. The truth was his female boss was a tornado and he was intimidated by her demands. Using my understanding that he was a feminine-minded gentle man, and she was a fierce masculine minded female, he gained an insight into how to deal with her. As she demanded his attention on a project, he would ask her the time frame and negotiate that by asking for time. He managed *her telling him*, by *asking* for time rather than hiding away. She knew he was totally reliable, accurate and would perform; and had previously doubted his command and decision making. Once they came to this understanding, she would fly off to her next meeting feeling confident in his work. The upshot was that they became best colleagues and had many more Magical Conversations about personal connections since they formed their working relationship. He remarked to me on our exit interview as we finished the coaching program, that he now understood her and she him. The core reason I was brought in to manage had melted away and his confidence made him stand head and shoulders above his colleagues quite literally!

Remember:

Your **RELATE-ability** is the natural evolution of your own grounded *sense of self as* key as you enter each Magical Conversation with loving intent. Your goal is to dissolve stuff and not get caught up in the rainstorm. As we **REACT,** take **RESPONSIBILITY** and recognize the **RISK** that is in front of us, we can enter these conversations and make the outcome right for all parties.

The major challenge in developing your practice of Magical Conversation is to let go of the past. The burden of the past can ruin your future success. To take **RESPONSIBILITY** is to practice letting go of negative history that often blocks the growth of your relationships. Holding on makes you weary. Sense the loving intention in every connection, relationship and deal, especially when negotiating deals and or talking over money or intimacy. The lessons learned already, however long you've been building a connection with someone, mount up like compound interest to trust and understand each other.

These clouds only hold the *STUFF*. Keep that in mind… STUFF equals UNIMPORTANT but needs sorting out. Remember that you are "in charge of YOU" and only YOU, and the chances are that you will experience success, endurance and joy if you develop your practice of Magical Conversations for serious topics and the resolution of difficulties as well as using the practice for 'out of the box' creativity and innovation.

The daily practice of the Value Principles become your behavior:

Speak with Authenticity: be yourself, do not wear a mask, every situation has two sides - an inside and an outside as well as your side and his/her/their side. Indeed, none of them are real. All are perceived by the beholder.

Develop Trust & respect: whatever the distress points are, you are human, have feelings, your presence even in an argument needs respect. Only through naming your issue and seeking honesty and integrity in response, can you build trust.

Seek Empathy: listen for their views genuinely and mindfully. No assumptions. No battles. Seek understanding through mutually respectful words.

Notice Balance: sense the ebb and flow of any issue. Seek to place it in the bigger context of your mutual world and the world at large.

Check Perceptions: everyone's is personal, and yours is real but not necessarily for the other person, all is perceived by the beholder.

Invite Perspectives: there can be many perspectives on any one issue. No one is right or wrong. It's dangerous territory to get into "I'm Right, you're wrong" and it has never won any mutuality contests!

Disclose with Transparency: see through to the other person's heart logic alongside head logic. Share your vulnerability, your natural response to each issue topic generally and from your point of view. Do not attack but do not be walked over.

Establish Clarity: think and reflect on words used, body language, touch and pause. Notice if your message has been received by watching for signs, verbal and non-verbal. Do not plead or beg; do not control or push your views on others. State your needs and expectations slowly and calmly, then pause and take a deep breath. Feel the energy in the space between you and others.

Value Compatibility: use the natural flow of loving intentions to seek compatibility, not sameness. Herein the magic is created. If dark clouds gather, hold firm to the compatibility you have been practicing and seek to complement the relationship you are building with another. Check in regularly that what you believe makes you compatible is what the other parties recognize too.

Practice, practice, practice

Remember your ultimate vision is a commitment to Magical Conversations without demands, yet, after an appropriate agreed time, with mutually beneficial actions to taken. Be sharing and caring, value inter-dependence as the best healthy option, enjoy dynamic joy and disruptive abundance, seek joy overcoming fear, be sure of your own mind, body and heart. You can win-win every time, even when not agreeing. Agree to disagree maybe but walk away without anger. I practice these principles every day.

Do I always get it right? NO!Do I do my best? YES.

Find your own practices that ground your soul and your belief in the magic. Magic is to believe the unbelievable occurs in front of your eyes.

My practices have developed over many decades and taught me that if, in my heart, I can say "I'm sorry, forgive me and thank you, I love you" then I find peace and grounded calmness in any situation that might throw me a curved ball!

This is a long-established Hawaiian mantra called **Ho'oponopono** - give thanks, talk of love, be sorry and forgive. This simple yet effective recital has healed deep wounds of rejection, even illness. It comes from the Hawaiian Tribes believe that this mantra or chant will heal their forefathers.

Forgiveness is the most powerful aid to love when crisis occurs. Look for your own daily support practices as there are many. Find ones that suit you. These apply to all aspects of life, business and personal. It may be meditation, breathing exercises, a class or therapy session, a walk in the park and stroll along the beach. Be kind to your self as you would be to others.

My passion to be a mediator and seeker of harmony has led me to understand that reactive judgements and anger make mutual resolution and happiness very hard to achieve. Over my lifetime of good experiences and some big hard-knocks moments, I discovered that my desire to create harmony, even in sad, angry or distressed moments, was always about my desire for harmony for myself as well as the other person/people involved. Random acts of kindness and showering the world with smiles just for the sake of happiness have been ideas that truly appeal to me all my life.

A Magical Conversation started my Latest Life Adventure

The morning of November 26th, 2011, I sat opposite a new acquaintance, James Omps, at a conference breakfast in Budapest, we had met the day before at the conference we attended and had caught that spark of connection that I mentioned earlier. We had chatted much of the day as we watched the speakers perform. It was, however, the next morning we had a 35-minute magical conversation. Why did this occur?

The fact that he was sitting in that corner table was maybe orchestrated by powers beyond our understanding. He was just finishing his meal and was about to leave had I not arrived.I had set and written intentions to meet my soulmate in my private journals, over the 16 years following my divorce. To this end, I was always ready to make the most of any opportunity to meet and converse with someone if I even had an inkling that my soul mate might appear right there in front of me at any moment.

Timing was key. The attraction was there.

We had spent the day before, during the initial joint session in the main body of the conference, chatting and sparking off regarding work and potential business ideas. As a masculine-minded business woman, I love to talk about and create potential business deals.

The chit-chat with a newfound friend and ally was welcomed in the middle of an exhausting conference schedule and had put us at ease but nothing more. This breakfast meeting was different. 35 minutes over eggs and bacon, we explored the far reaches of the universe, from galaxy to galaxy and back again. We shared more deeply than most male-female first-meeting experiences.

I found myself joyful, being transparent, and genuinely engaged, telling him things that people don't usually share. We shared values, passions, and legacy visions, stories of families and even talk of aliens and time travel too. We talked of sadness and departure and he shared the fact that his current wife had packed up and left him a month prior. He also talked with fondness about his long-term previous marriage relationship of 37 years to the mother of his 5 children. As we talked, he told me stories he had never shared with a stranger.

I recounted my divorce 16 years earlier, my ex-husband's steady decline in health, my grown-up children and grandchildren, my enduring sadness over the loss of my mother who had died suddenly in the summer of the year. I touched on the fact that, upon my return to England, I was destined to become nomad within a week as I had to leave my flat-share. I also mentioned that, while I was not overly concerned, my situation was causing quite a stir between my adult children, who were quite concerned about my obvious lack of focus as they saw it.

It was an extraordinary choice point in my life and there was this handsome loving man, single and in-tune with me, sitting with blue eyes twinkling as he smiled at my every word. I didn't think any further than this was truly a Magical Conversation and so I shared my ideas on this concept and why I felt it worked with him. He was intrigued. I was used to connecting with business men and women with ease; seeing men as friends and just like me, a business person. This time, however, it was more than that… much deeper and more personal than normal. It was not a 'chat up' session either.

He is Jim, my husband now, and is a gentle *feminine*-minded introvert man, the *gender dynamics* type that appealed to me as a counter balance to my tom-boy *masculine*-minded femaleness. As I came to know in our relationship, shared later that he had been truly amazed at how easy it was to talk to me about some clearly challenging issues for him. He had had cancer, had chemo, radiation therapy, nearly died, but survived. He felt safe to share and I honored to be that space holder. Kindness, compassion, empathy and willingness to hear another's being tuned into you was my mantra that day. It was the right place, the best space, I was ready. Trust in yourself, that you are worthy and that your *Magical Love Cconversation* may turn up any time. Just be ready!!

I didn't foresee in that moment that within a year we'd be married and, that 6 years later, would have lived in Malaysia for 4 years, on a different continent, Asia-Pacific. Now, in 2018, we're in California, a new continent for me. I didn't know, nor did he, that we would be where we are today, sharing the adventure of a lifetime, launching this book and another soon after, venturing onto live screen and online programs, and building the power to assure that legacy we spoke of that time six-plus years ago. We are ready to change the world if the world is ready to listen. Our legacy statement was then and is now "to leave the world a better place for having been here".

Was I a stranger that morning? Was he? We shared the feeling that we had known each other forever… perhaps in another place or another time? There was no intimacy, no kiss, merely the joy of Magical Conversations, considerable fun and genuine laughter as we sat through the morning's conference program.

Three hours later, we exchanged business cards shortly before I left for the airport. Then, a wistful goodbye, a soft, reassuring squeeze of the arm and a goodbye peck on the cheek, a professional farewell and a spoken promise to one day work together. I walked away wondering how that could possible transpire? London… Las Vegas? That is a very long commute!!!

After 6 months and 45,000 words in emails between us, we had gotten to know considerably more about each other, and eventually confessed our growing love for one another. I flew to Las Vegas on May 21, 2012. Our first kiss confirmed that I had met my soulmate.

Has the journey been smooth? No. Exciting? Yes. Rewarding? Definitely.

I tell my story to share that when you are prepared to attract Magical Conversations, anything can happen. Through my practice, I have gained a new awareness of how Magical Conversations can help us grow in prosperity, not merely wealth but life's legacy of love and happiness too.

Understanding Jim's ill-health after surgery, our residing in a new country, with our new and growing relationship, an irregular cash flow, relatively high cost, using our wits, finding work, this adventure has been challenging and rewarding and a tale to share in another book maybe? Life is all about possibilities and choices, values and beliefs that can change your journey of understanding and new habits that can form if you decide to allow loving intentions and Magical Conversations to work for you as a changemaker choice for your life.

A Formula for Successful Magical Conversations - No Judgement, No Anger, No Controlling Actions – Be Open minded, Joyful, Mindful and Flowing, come from your heart not your head (listen to your thoughts in alignment within your experience).

Developing Magical Conversations into a way of life for personal and professional goals has helped me to magnetize my message and monetize my conversations. Now I share this formula with you, one that I know will transform your business and your life. You can 'pull' success to you rather than 'push' to sell yourself. Make way for magic and the magnetic pull of prosperity and happiness.

This is how I have evolved the Magical Conversations formula as an intentional strategy for life and for business. It's one-part Pure Magic and three parts Authenticated Conversational Principles set out here. It's all about bringing something of yourself to a conversation; something that comes from your heart and is moderated by the mind. Your truth is important when words and deeds are aligned. The experience of YOU with others is key. Once you have prepared yourself as described throughout this book, you have set your loving intentions and got to know yourself, then you are ready to proceed.

Invite people to a Magical Conversation (officially)

Magical Conversations can be an organized gathering or an instantaneous meet up with family and friends. I ran Magical Conversation Circles for the last 8 years in the UK and in Malaysia. The organized circles are time bound (2-3 hours - enough to brew amazing creativity), and contributors are invited. The same rules apply in all situations. The outcomes are creative thoughts, ideas, learning, shifting perspectives, knowledge, imagination sparks and practical solutions found that can be acted on later. The topic in the middle of the table is the focus not the personalities or what people do, it's what they can give to conversation that creates what matters. Experiences shared will lead us to learn about others, joyful sharing brings love and happiness into the experience. Yet the focus is the topic not the people, the results enhance all lives even if the points each take away are different. Remember it is the experience and the feeling that you will enjoy as much as the content. In practice, invite someone to note ideas and statements in a random mind-map collation, this serves as a pictorial reminder and must not be a 'to-do' list!

This works for personal conversations that you'd like to wave some magic onto. Decide which topic is to be discussed, start with the positive rainbow intentions especially if dealing with the *stuff* of your clouds. Ensure your vehicle (your body, mind and heart) is valuable to you and make sure you have the best fuel in your engine and, where possible, arrange the best time for the other person/s to be in the conversation. Be in the right mind frame, breathe and inhale loving thoughts before commencing. Ensure you create a loving space, light airy, sit side by side, or opposite each other, in a comfortable at ease manner, in a circle if you have choice. If the physical environment is challenged by *stuff,* then do your best to create a *safe* space to talk. Eliminate as many noises and distractions as possible. Make sure the other/s in your conversational space are well and make them feel safe to contribute.

Ensure all parties hear and are clear of the rules. State that there are **No Judgements** allowed and invite all to avoid assumptions. Encourage an open mind and a values-based conversation. State your values simply in your welcome, appropriately. For example, "it is a pleasure to be here, let's share our experiences and value our differences in a mindful manner". Add descriptors appropriate to your goals. Is it a serious topic, a creative exploration, a personal issue, or business process? It may be any topic, the rules apply.

Use your own experiences and viewpoints and share with authenticity and clarity. Set your own standards consistently. Invite your own perspective to be respected as your unique perceptions of any situation. At the same time respect other's perspectives as theirs. Be open minded. By engaging in this way, we honor each other and especially our different behavior dynamics as men and women, of different generations, culture and sexual orientations. Aim to understand all who enter the space you create and allow others to share within your welcome. Your objective is to guide not control. Do set a time dimension appropriately so you can manage the contribution timeline before any actions need to occur. Actions come after the Magical Conversation has evolved its magic!

Say everything **Without Anger** or any meanness; breathe deeply before you start, enroll his or her attention, set these intentions and honor all parties. Bring mindful joy and energy to the space you all share and the words that are beginning to flow. Preparation is key.

1. Prepare your mind, heart and body before you start. Breathe in with the word love in your mind. Think, experience, and be open hearted in your intention. Share from your experiences not opinions.

2. Settle your body into a mindful state. Keep loving memories in your heart and recognize the emotional bank balance between you and the differences that will make your connection work well. Take care with your body language and lean into listen.

3. Listen, listen, listen, and then speak to first check your understanding when offered the opportunity. Speak from your heart, spare lovingly and consciously. Do not interrupt or start until sure the space between you holds your mutual loving intentions.

Finally, have **No Controlling Actions** or overt pressure or urgency to decide or draw a conclusion until all are ready and the time is closed. Don't make promises you might not be able to keep.

Respect time and pressure influence: Do not put a control or any urgency such as "you must…" command into any conversation you wish to be magical. This will affect the flow.

Observe Diversity and Dynamics

Before and during the Magical Conversation itself, be aware of the differences that people bring with them i.e. their gender dynamics, their generational experiences, their sexual orientation, their abilities or impairments and their cultural and ethnic history. Diversity is a vital essence in the magic mix and needs careful consideration in every conversation.

Note carefully the fundamental differences between men and women as a starter. This is my major focus in working with clients. I study their natural gender dynamics and attributes in conversation styles.

Men generally tend to converse in *boxes* one topic at a time, with a task focused linear approach. This *"either or"* style can bring a limit to a free flow conversation while women generally converse in *circles*, multi-tasking, nurturing and 'feeling' their way to relationships and results. This is what I call an *"and - and"* approach to conversations.

Within each gender biology, there is a range of *masculine to feminine* traits that occur and can be witnessed in different behavioral approaches to conversations. Remember my tom-boy masculine mind? My core conversation style is grounded in my female nature, i.e. *circular* and *relationship* focused, however my mindset is logical, thinking, task focused and seeking collaboration for solutions required. This latter style is more *boxed* straight-line, masculine, in process. My conversation style can err to this more *masculine* behavior and may be received as over direct and male (but I am not a male!) Men and women range in conversational style along a *masculine - feminine* axis within each gender biology/physicality, in addition to *male and female* preferences for conversation.

My style is a Masculine-minded Female, I call this MF, my husband Jim, as I described him to you, is a gentle intuitive male, a Feminine-minded Male FM. Men range in style from his to a more Masculine-minded Male MM, action man style. Women range in style from mine to a more Feminine-minded female FF, more detailed focused, verbally dexterous and intuitive. In studying my own style and physicality during the last 30 years, I observed that our body skeleton and stance also played a part in our presence and demeanor.

These observations led me to understand and create a 360° perspective over and above the two-dimensional biological divide *'male – female'* axis. I realized to understand more I had to assess and map the core driver differences and add a *'masculine – feminine'* axis. The physicality behavior range is added into each biological territory. The map is a deeper application of factors already known from writers such as Dr John Gray "Men are from Mars, Women are from Venus" in which he writes similarly of the two core territories you see in my Gender Dynamics© Map illustrated here, the *box* (male Mars) and the *circle* (female Venus) are my visual shapes to help you recognize core differences.

The additional drill-down in my studies, born from my own experiences and observations of 100s of men and women over last 20 years, is that physicality (bone structure and stance) shows an alignment to potential behavioral characteristics. The straighter the structure of the body, and the more angular the features, the more likely the male or female with those features will use *masculine* style behaviors such as *logic, processing, thinking, linear thinking*. Like myself, in my tomboy straight stance and skeleton, I knew I was female yet not as *feminine* as many females I knew. Likewise, softer bone structures and stance indicated *feminine* behaviors, softer approaches, *e.g. more intuitive traits and verbal dexterity*. These behaviors are not indicators of sexual orientations at all. It merely allows for females having masculine-minds and males having feminine-minds. Every sexual orientation, LBGT is on the map as this maps behavior and the dynamics that occur for all human beings as they relate to others. If you are a male, you are in the range MM-M -FM, if a female, in the range MF-F-FF in a 360° perspective. If T then you may move across from M-F, or F-M.

My years in business have helped me understand these ranges and design this Gender Dynamics© Map to apply to every situation where people relate to each other. This map enables you to navigate a diverse group of styles when you are in conversation. I have worked with this map with 100's of clients to start their awareness conversation not to label them. Knowing where you start, who's around your table and what communication route to take with other types aids your best chances for magnetic Magical Conversations.

For an ease of understanding the basic differences, the most important attribute to be aware of between men and women is that the men generally chatter less and work systematically in *boxes*, one topic at a time.

The Gender Dynamics© Map 2018

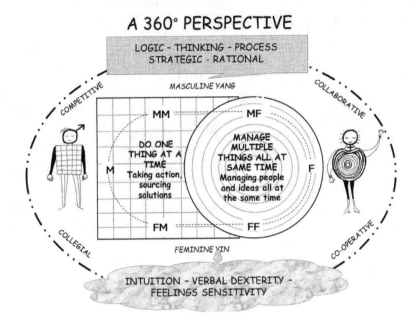

A 360° PERSPECTIVE

Women generally flow in *circles* of conversation and tangential yet intertwined messages. Women tend ask questions without always needing answers, men tend to ask questions and hear questions as tasks to be resolved.

There is more information available in my online programs and in my book; The Gender Dynamics of Life and Love -Who's in Charge? To be published January 2019 www.missmagicalconversations.com

Here are a few Gender Dynamics observations to be aware of as you engage in Magical Conversations.

Men Be Aware: women need to have time to state their feelings over and over, circular in nature. When they ask questions, they do not need a solution too quickly even if they appear to be asking for one. Use positive affirmations, repeat any compliments honestly, hold an appreciative gaze, and remember she is NOT in a box.

She enjoys being able to tend or befriend. She cares, that is why an issue you see in the cloud, she may see in the rainbow. Some women may be more likely to be logical (MF) and get challenging, responding with an energy that appears to say, "I can do without you." Some on the other hand, may turn inward if you're insensitive and bend her wings (FF). Females often like to get things off their chest and once delivered feel better, while if the man is drowning emotionally he may not ask for a life-line!

Women Be Aware: men cannot often take too much chatter and emotion without being stranded in their "either/or" solution focused BOX.

Men may want to bring a solution to you if you are distressed and especially if they feel they are the cause of your distress. He wants to help and cannot find a solution that he believes is right for you so it's painful whoever appears to him on the attack (his viewpoint if you're crying as a woman). You feel your emotions like a river torrent, he *receives* it like a tornado of anguish and does not know how to quell it. He fights of flights! The MM nature may get impatient with you and the FM may disappear into his cave or computer!

Yin – Yang
The conversation balance
is in your hands, male,
female, masculine,
feminine, all differences
count as blessings.

8

MAGNETIZE YOUR MAGICAL CONVERSATIONS

Monetize your Message and Win Business

YOUR **Pot of Gold is at The End of YOUR Rainbow…**

The rainbow is where your mutual intentions with others come alive in a Magical Conversation. Set personal intentions to be magical within yourself before entering the conversation. Do share and agree the rules openly with others so they own the mutuality too. For business as in life success, the same rules and loving intentions, principles and assessments as laid out in this book, apply.

Make sure you value yourself, your practice of knowing YOU is maximized by following the guidelines and principles in this book. Ensure *The Value Creation Cycle* evolves from your heart center not your head logic. Keep your Relational Quotient on top form, with daily workouts as you understand your personal 4Rs and study others who are different to you. Be OK with differences; therein lies the magic fusion!

Know your Passion, Communication Choices, Asset and Vulnerabilities. Add them all to your personal growth plans and know them deep within you. You are now a walking-talking magnet and ready for action.

As a magnet you attract or repel depending on how YOU place the magnet towards others. You know the force of a positive magnet, once connected it stays strong. As you practice the loving intention of this Magical Conversation style of communication, you will be ready to bond not only with family and friends and your intimate soulmate, you can also attract clients and business deals to enhance your prosperity.

If you run your own business, careful and consistent development of your **Value Creation Cycle**, and devoted time on the lessons in this book, will add to your magical credentials in whatever service you offer. You're ready to monetize your conversations for a deal, a sale, a joint venture or a long-term prosperity partnership by not pushing but *pulling*. Switch on the magnet power and follow the rules, people will enjoy being connected to you as you empower them to join into your magic.

It may be that you are an employee on a rising career path, YOUR understanding of what is occurring around you as you lead conversations at team meetings or in the boardroom matter for your success. Watch the chatter generally in the corridors of your workspace and develop your profile as a Magical Conversations enthusiastic employee and you will get noticed – for the right reasons. In business, shared dialogue and rapport building are critical attributes as you rise through the organization. Today there are many challenges in the workplace where men and women sometimes battle for power, you can become the magnet for a new way to converse that others may not have experienced.

You may be the leader, the boss, male or female, who wants to inspire a mixed management team of men and women and create the best culture that embraces all parties. Other diverse factors make up your workforce and Magical Conversation Circle events are an ideal way to bring often delicate or contentious issues into a safe zone. By following the rules, the magic works as everyone shares without judgement, anger or controls. I have run such sessions and am always very grateful for the creative content that arises. My intention is to create the right space, to adhere to the rules, and to allow human beings natural wisdom to arise. *Loving intentions in the workplace* are underrated assets and this experience works as many people need to be heard and often are fearful to speak. As the rules become a natural part of people's lives, with loving intentions as the magic wand, difficult subjects and situations can be overcome.

I have worked with many difficult situations with business clients, my remit is to sort out 'bad behavior'. This is particularly acute with the current climate of sexual harassment cases being a lurking threat. CEOs need to develop mixed diverse cultures where differences are honored and inappropriate behavior is overcome by staff developing a mutually owned moral compass. I have worked with many clients on these issues. In my experience with clients it is the unspoken fears that harm, and cause boundaries to be crossed often unconsciously. The turnaround comes when people realized they are all asked to create the new environment of healthy collaborative working.

Collective ownership of a work place culture is key to collaboration, the leaders may set the product or service values for the company, but a wise leader engages his or her staff in owning these values in their hearts. My UK company is called Corporate Heart and it does just that; it delivers programs and products that ensure the heart of every employee beats well and increases profit through collective performance efforts. Let me give you an example. I designed a major engagement program for a car distributor network in the UK, the wide spread nature of the network had made for a fragmented work ethos. Bringing staff together into a Magical Conversation Circles and setting topics that built trust and respect was a powerful engagement process and enabled everyone to get involved. It shifted the energy of the business landscape for all parties, managers, mechanics, sales teams, and administration.

"The engagement sessions rolled out across the Express Fit Dealerships were brilliantly designed to capture the essence of the key message "Adding Value". Our requirement was to shift 'hearts and minds' of everyone delivering our 'Express Fit' service. I was personally amazed that such a short session can create a great deal of energy, honest sharing and commitment to action ....and gave everyone a new sense of personal value within the business!" *Julie Rosser, Manager-Workshop Programmes, Peugeot Express Fit dealership*

Bring your magic to work!

Observe who is around your circle, at your table, in your deal. Are they the MM, strong boxed, directive? Are they FM, servant leaders, intuitive feelings-type men? Are they MF, strong forceful, logical women, or FF caring, sensitive and nurturing? Attracting, connecting and building relationships with all types are keys to you gaining faithful clients, customers, a community and a loyal tribe.

Make sure 70% plus of your words and actions in any exchange are positive and embracing each person engaged. Then factor in your wisdom to manage the 30% that is the unknown, the challenging or confusing. You are building the rapport to make issues easier to work through. Know when to listen and when to speak. The results you desire will emerge as you flow together, and you realize the rainbow intentions that overarch throughout the initial engagement process of shared experiences and the continued Magical Conversations you practice in the lifetime of every relationship.

Remember to connect at a heart-center level first (not head), communicate based on the principles we have covered, and created conversations that flow, engaging everyone's styles and diversity factors. You are the host of your own Magical Conversations so set the scene, build the atmosphere and guide others without them knowing, embrace loving intentions and the experience you create will bring forth the results you desire.

Here is a summary list to guide you as you become an expert at your own Magical Conversations.

Setting the Scene

1. Set intentions rather than expectations

2. Guide the conscious unifying purpose of the conversation and honor all participants

3. Decide the mutual topic/s and underlying scenario with consent and within the purpose as agreed

4. Agree on core principles: no anger, no judgement, no urgency, pressure or stress

5. Define mindful goals with no overt persuasion to action unless organic and mutually agreed

6. Give all permission to speak and observe core polite etiquette

7. Create the best listening environment and respectful trust to all, sitting in a circle where ever available, use an open space and clear desks where possible in work environments

8. Facilitate an energy flow, time keeping and monitoring the space as safe and sacred to the conversation at hand

9. Oversee the process without control, seeking inclusion and collaboration

10. Where appropriate, charter the conversation output on paper, unattributed to any one person and in a mind-map display

The Results for You and Others and Your Business.

If you are creating an invitation for a scheduled Magical Conversation Circle and new parties are curious as to why this will benefit the participants, you might wish to share the following as potential reasons to individuals and groups. These are the results that my clients have reported to me after the formal experience:

1. Getting your true voice heard without being rebuffed

2. Being confident to share and learn at the same time

3. Being unafraid to comment on sensitive and serious topics

4. Enjoying the potential widening of perspectives and perceptions

5. Growing a far broader based knowledge of other's views

6. Gathering 'ah ha' awareness on any chosen variety of topics

7. Making connections and collaborations based on people's individual values, authenticity, and trust

8. Furthering creative opportunities for business and life on a local and global scale

Bonus Results as you expand your Business Operations with a Magical Conversation Forum or Circle

As a leader in your own business or in a corporation, you will find that the scheduling of formal sessions sets the scene for;

- Building a cohesive co-creative team

- Ensuring a more flexible inspirational leadership style

- Embedding a collaborative and empowered inclusive work cultures

- Seeding unexpected opportunities and ideas that bring profitability and sustainability

- Smoother operational and professional relationships and co-operation among your people

At the end of the day, my experience is that people would rather live and work in a loving environment than one built on fear. People feel great when they feel their voice and contribution counts, and when they do, they create better business results all round and profits grow exponentially!

This testimonial is a great joy to me from the example I share earlier of a special Magical Conversation Circle in central London...

"Pauline is inspirational! I had the rare privilege of being involved in one of her Magical Conversations in London, together with a group of distinguished business leaders. Her emotional maturity and calm, but persuasive leadership style, is quite something to behold. But what makes Pauline unique is her deep understanding of feminine energy and intuition present in most organizations, but often suppressed by more domineering masculine energy. In a world where we seem to have got so many things wrong, Pauline's approach to business is a welcome and refreshing lifeline."

Mike Haupt, CEO, Noetic Business

I have personally designed and hosted many hundreds of Magical Conversations, for senior leaders, male and female, to explore and share their viewpoints, possibilities and visions, enabling new solutions to emerge. This has been across the UK, Asia Pacific and now the USA. The Gender Dynamics© Map is the science within the practice of Magical Conversations. The practice produces amazing results that ensures people work better and so profits go up and costs go down; it reduces arbitration and provides damage control mechanisms when inappropriate actions can cause disaster not just for company reputations but for people's lives.

The growth of a Magical Conversations culture is like refuelling your car with high octane gas. Today the workforce is highly technical, digitally connected, entrepreneurial and a healthy diverse balance of men and women. As I develop leaders and help them to manage both their own destiny and their own lives as well as their workforce, I find that these organizations become more aware of the broader social issues, Corporate Social Responsibility, setting new moral ethics and business etiquette, and connecting with community issues that surround their business. From the results of these Magical Conversations come many bright ideas, innovative products and a collaborative learning as to how to lead on new ideas and issues in the boardroom and in team meetings.

My passion is to help people and businesses to build conversations that matter and take actions that make the difference to people and profits. If we are going to create a new future, the story starts now!

As you seek to become a magnet that attracts the best clients and customers, you will more easily monetize your own conversations, whether in your own business or on your career progression. Do not focus on money even though financial gain is the result. Focus on the relationship and the messages, the energy and the connection. You need first to be loving in your intentions, seek to understand others, build rapport with a high relational quotient, value differences, and create Magical Conversations that embrace all parties. These conversations will take you into the unknown. Be ready for the unexpected deal, the contract that swells your bank balance, and an outcome that delivers an infinite range of possibilities that you never imagined. That is magic!

Welcome to your magic, have some serious fun and enjoy the journey. YOU are 'in charge' of YOU and the impact you can create in other people's lives and your own is in your hands.

---

*"Value and love your life first so that you can impact others appropriately with loving intentions. **We** will be formed by **You** and **I'** ... and the only person you can ever truly know is the **'I am** within. Use this as your daily mantra for a balanced life, a magical conversation practice and abundant success in all matters of the heart. I have and I know it works!"*

... Dr Pauline Crawford-Omps

The pot of gold is at the end of YOUR rainbow. Set intentions and make welcome the magical conversation within you. Enjoy the journey to success.

EPILOGUE

Bears or Birds - Who's in Charge?
A Magical Story of Changing Times

In the search for a new understanding and a Magical Conversation between men and women, let's take an oblique perspective and a story of many new possibilities using the unlikely metaphor of bears (men) and birds (women) to tackle a challenged business world and the economic chaos we might see today.

Maybe there are two different cultures rapidly merging, two natures, one vision? Maybe this story is not so unlikely?

Once upon a time... the business *City* had been built over many decades on the "square mile" principle; every inch measurable and maximized for the owners, each square inch sold and resold, marked up, traded down; every skyscraper fielded a magnificent view yet many streets were cold from the deep shadows the towers made. The inner streets were paved with gold and had a labyrinth of tunnel journeys and caves connected by long corridors, lift shafts and stairs and out of this a very hard-nosed culture had grown. This *City* was inhabited by the Bears.

There was another *City*, known more as a *Community* – hidden away over those past decades. This was designed to be a community culture, with open landscape, cosy rooms, and play stations for the younger members to learn and flourish, nesting nooks for conversations, space for innovation and creativity coffee breaks; here there were support systems that shared resources and

reduced waste. This inner city was a mesh of inter-connected live wires and tree top nests. This inner community was inhabited by the Birds.

The Bears and the Birds were well known to each other as they had shared the earth together for millenniums, breathing the same air, drinking the same water, eating up the same resources; however they needed different things, they had different biological needs, and even though they often held similar aspirations and dreams for their future, their perspectives on how that came to be where subtly different.

Their challenge was to understand each other as the two cities grew side by side, and business and life began to interweave. Over the last decades where viral changes, technology and flexible ways of working and living had become blended in style, some top-level Bears observed their world was changing and surrounding market and social boundaries collapsing, evolving, and revolving in ever decreasing circles. Many natural and economic disasters challenged the very foundations of the world that both Bears, and Birds loved. They now faced a world-in-crisis and obstacles that threatened to undermine life as previously known.

The Bears continued to prowl their *City*. Some were gruff, grizzly and dangerous; some were strong and proud of their mighty presence; others were young cub Bears who were learning from their elders; some were afraid of their own shadows and yet many acted like teddy Bears, warm and cuddly, keen to protect and nurture their young.

The Birds were very different to the Bears; many variable types withplumes of many coloured feathers, bodies of different sizes and wing spans spread to glide and soar; big and small, wild and tame; some flew in formation, others lived as family units, others fought their own battles, while many twittered happily over the garden wall. They all sang beautiful and creative songs. However, once they were attacked, damaged or caught on the ground or attacked by Bears, the Birds were terrified. Losing a limb, a wing, or a feather made them victims.

Some Birds learned to adapt to business and became even "terrifying" to the Bears; they swooped and soared; they preyed on the most vulnerable; the cub Bear often headed for the caves when he saw a vicious Bird coming. Many Birds sang from their hearts and were full of the sweet evening song of common sense, the sound of their voices infiltrated the airwaves of business and life as they travelled to and from work and home (as home was very precious to them) and they grew in numbers as the scent of financial independence made them flutter and flourish.

Increasingly the Birds started invading the Bear's *City* (where the Bears had regularly inhabited for their daily work) seeking bigger worms and prospects for their life's survival. They realized there were rich pickings for them too. It was tough going for the Birds to begin with as the Bears were big and strong. They had built their *City* to be the powerhouse that generated wealth and provided resources for their own caves. Their traditions were well embedded in their mind-set. They like to come home to their home nesting Birds. They didn't always approve of working Birds. They made it a perilous journey for many working Birds, who tried to perch on the higher levels of the skyscrapers, looking for safe habitats and life-saving perches.

Many Bears didn't want the Birds to get into their work spaces and high-rise hard -earned stakes; however, the Birds were determined that they were there to stay and grew in numbers every year. The more conscious wise Birds and Bears knew that, for the survival of their species, the only way forward would be together.

The Bears could not understand why Birds talked in circles, chattered with others and used seemingly random tangents to think through problems. Bears thought and acted in boxes, directed in straight lines and expected solutions to every question. The Birds longed to bring their circular birdsong to be truly valued and honoured by the Bears as an intrinsic and valuable part of a fulfilled and successful work-life balance. After all, they valued the Bears for their strength, tenacity, logical thinking and especially their ability to be the major provider to the family. The Birds loved the adoration that the Bears gave them at home and in many communities where they nurtured their families of young Bears and Birds.

Once more and more Birds had discovered *The City* that the Bears have created, they wanted a bigger piece of the worm pie. They knew they could add new value, natural skills, more emotional intelligence, a good relationship management and different consumer knowledge to that which the Bears had. They knew they could deliver much of what the Bears offered yet with a nurturing inclusive spirit that would sustain better long-term results; combining a healthier lifestyle alongside the tradition fiscal success. Yet given all that the Birds brought to the Bear's *City*, the gateways to the high skyscrapers often proved difficult and had closed combination locks that barred the doorways to the boardroom.

Can the Bears and the Birds sing a new Magical Conversation song together?

Now times have changed. The internet highway, global trade, business from your home, education for all and entrepreneurship have all blossomed and the Birds are flourishing too and sing their beautiful songs and lyrics even more than ever. Their activities, especially the younger Y and X Gen, and now Millennium *Bears and Birds* are creating new cultures and different perspectives that are meaningful and inclusive.

Of course, some wise Bears and Birds are now getting together and writing tunes of collaboration with cords of perfection to sooth the noisy chaotic world. More and more come to share the Magical Conversations that arise. These species from all generations want to bring a new harmonic to the service repertoire of business but still some older more traditional Bears don't understand these songs. When they try to sing along, their deep voices threaten the very nature of the Bird song.

The Bears often get stuck with their macho 'pow-wow' power groups and warrior sports games. Some Bears learn to be emotional.

The Bears and the Birds seem at odds with each other yet there is also an intimate attraction between them; Bears and Birds love each other and have done since the beginning of time. When the attraction flourishes, they form families to parent new generations of Birds and Bears. Indeed, they naturally complement each other.

Can the Bears really let the Birds into The City in ways that truly integrate the needs of both? Can the Birds persuade the Bears to get together and co-create a new domain that integrates business and life, economic revival and social cohesion?

Is it "business bliss, boom or bust?"

Will bear-growl or bird-song win? Only time would tell. The end of the story is still being written… maybe Magical Conversations is the key to our future pot of gold?

ABOUT THE AUTHOR

Dr. Pauline Crawford-Omps

President, World Association of Visioneers & Entreprenologists

Miss Magical Conversations, International Speaker, Gender Dynamics© Expert, Image Consultant and Changemaker.

Pauline is a 30-year business consultant and professional facilitator of transformational programs, with a wide range of corporate clients in Corporate UK, Asia Pacific and US. Her life adventure has taken her round the world. She took a major step change in November 2011 when she met and fell in love with her Soul Mate, American Veteran, Jim, at a conference in Budapest, Hungary. Their magical conversation led to an extraordinary love adventure. She from the UK, he from US, they married in October 2012 in Las Vegas. Their course of true love however was beset by challenges of Jim's ill-health with two major operations in the first year of marriage. They left their home countries for his recovery to live in Malaysia for 4 years where Pauline worked with many clients from education and government organizations. Arriving in California on Dec 31st 2017, Pauline and Jim are now stepping onto a new path. Their mission to establish harmony between men and women in all walks of life, love and business, is core to Magical Conversations.

A well-known UK speaker since the 90's, Pauline designed The Gender Dynamics© Map to enable women and men to come together in a clear understanding of their differences. This innovative tool lays out the baseline to create personal and professional relationships that make a difference to life success at work and at home. Pauline has spoken on stages across the world.

Sociologist/Statistics Graduate, Business Psychologist, Image Consultant, Magical Conversations Host, MBA and PhD in Entreprenology, CEO and Founder Corporate Heart Ltd, a UK based Performance Consultancy since 1999. Founder of Gender Dynamics International US, President of the World Association of Visioneers and Entreprenologists, Chairperson of Permanent Commission on Social Issues and Women Entrepreneurship, WUSME (World Union of Small & Medium Enterprises), and Program Director, International University of Entreprenology.

Contact Pauline on pauline@missmagicalconversations.com

www.missmagical conversations.com

Mastering Magical Conversations Program (online)

Certified Ambassador of Magical Conversations

This is a Six-Step Online Interactive Program, including Video Recordings, Workbooks, Assignments Webinars and Zoom Coaching Sessions – 1-Value Creation, 2-Gender Dynamics, 3-Relational Quotient, 4-Partnerships & Principles, 5-Magnetize & Monetize, 6-Business & Life Growth

Programs available

SOULMATE LOVE

Inviting men and/or women of all ages ready for love

Are you ready for the language of love? Whether you are looking to flourish or find anew, **SoulMateLove** is for you. This program experience enhances your chances as you receive **A Code of Love** identification system, and the means to discover and/or sustain your life partner. You can absolutely discover, develop and attract life-long love and happiness into your life.

MEN OF THE FUTURE NOW

An exclusive program for professional men

You are the role model for the man of the future. Events are influencing and determining how a MAN will function in both professional and social environments. If you want to be ahead of the curve rather than working overtime to catch up, **Men of the Future** will give you the roadmap to take you from here to your future success with ease.

WOMEN OF SIGNIFICANCE TODAY

An exclusive program for professional women

The need for women to step forward is paramount but it is going to take more than boldness. Beginning with determined and designed, **Women of Significance** is going to take your female leadership of the highest order. This program provides a guide and support systems that you can use to chart your path to being one of those leaders, being a woman of significance.

GENDER COLLABORATION

Exclusively for men and women in top management

Are you ready to gain the business advantage in virtually all business circles?

If you are ready to navigate the winning team, this is your opportunity to get the map that can take you from Point A to Point B without wasting your time. **Gender Collaboration** and **The Gender Dynamics© Map** unlock top level success.

Contact Pauline@missmagicalconversations.com

CPSIA information can be obtained
at www.ICGtesting.com
Printed in the USA
FFHW010012140319
50968027-56399FF